Frontispiece: Few photographs convey the size of the Forth Bridge, but here the ex-N.B.R. 'Scott' 4-4-0 and its train are truly dwarfed

Science Museum

The Pre-Grouping Railways

Their development, and individual characters

Part 3

Christine Heap

John van Riemsdijk

London: Her Majesty's Stationery Office

© Crown copyright 1985

First published 1985

ISBN 0 11 290432 7

Contents

List of Illustrations

In Colour:

The above illustrations, with the exception of 'v', are from paintings by Patricia F. Walker of the Science Museum Design Studio, based on contemporary photographs.

Black and White:

Maps:

I A North British country mixed train, circa 1914. Train engine designed by W. P. Reid. A Holmes goods locomotive in the background

II A McIntosh 'Dunalastair 2nd' northbound with a mixture of the best Caledonian and West Coast Joint Stock

III The celebrated 'Cardean' leaving Glasgow on the Corridor. A Conner 2-4-0 starts a local train on the left

IV Light engine on the Glasgow & South Western. One of the pretty but hard working Manson 4-4-0s on its way to pilot the Diner

V Pickersgill 4-4-0 No. 115, Great North of Scotland Railway

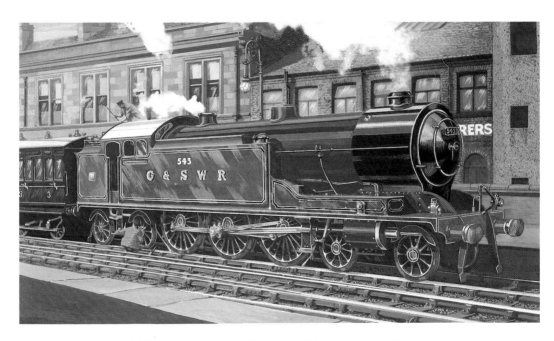

VI The last great Scottish locomotive design. A Whitelegg 'Baltic' at Glasgow St. Enoch

VII One of Cumming's Highland Railway 'Clan' 4-6-0s still in pre-Grouping colours around 1924. The West Coast Joint Stock diner is already in L.M.S. maroon

Introduction

James Watt was a Scotsman. He did not actually invent the steam engine but he improved it out of recognition by the application of scientific principles being newly worked out in Scotland, notably by Professor Black, his chief at Glasgow University. And he made it relatively economical and so far more generally useful.

Later, in the great age of railway building in the nineteenth century, formal engineering education at university level was not to be had in England, but it flourished in Scotland, and the preliminary education of Scottish students equipped them very well for serious study. Small wonder, then, that Scottish engineers spread over the world: railway engineers, civil engineers, and above all marine engineers. And they still do.

Britain's greatest ocean liners were built on the Clyde, and there also was the greatest concentration of locomotive building in the days of steam, including not only the Cowlairs works of the North British Railway and the St. Rollox works of the Caledonian, but also the three private building firms of Sharp, Stewart at the Atlas Works; Neilson at the Hyde Park Works, and Dubs at Queen's Park—all in Glasgow. The three private firms amalgamated in the first years of the twentieth century to form the North British Locomotive Company. The products of these three works were to be found all over the globe.

Scottish railway engineers who came south to work in England were far more numerous than their representation among the locomotive superintendents or chief mechanical engineers might suggest. The real designers of locomotives were often the chief draughtsmen, men like Walter Mackersie Smith of the N.E.R. (and the Midland Compounds) and Jock Anderson of the Midland. But some reached the top: Dugald Drummond and Robert Urie on the London & South Western, Patrick Stirling on the Great Northern, and others including Patrick's relative James on the South Eastern and Matthew on the Hull & Barnsley. There were few Englishmen who held such eminence on a Scottish railway, save in the very early years, but one who did was William Stroudley from Oxfordshire, who founded a school of design which culminated in the products of Drummond and McIntosh on the Caledonian, and those of Holmes and Reid on the North British.

Another school of Scottish locomotive design arose later, on the Highland and the Glasgow & South Western, and equally probably in the drawing offices of the Atlas Works of Sharp, Stewart and Co. This school either derived from or contributed to the design of locomotives for overseas, which were a main part of Sharp, Stewart's business and one in which information was necessarily shared with its neighbours, Neilson and Dubs, even before the three amalgamated. It is almost impossible now to decide whether the firms influenced the railways' engineers, or whether the former derived some of their ideas from the latter. Also, the railway company engineers were often employed as consultants by the overseas railways for which locomotives were being built.

This new Scottish school was exemplified first in the Highland goods 4-6-0s of 1894—the 'Jones Goods'—the first 4-6-0s built for a British main line railway. David Jones of the

Highland had a chief draughtsman named D. A. Hendrie, an ex-pupil who had spent time with Sharp, Stewart and Dubs, and who was later to be a great chief mechanical engineer of the South African Railways. He and Jones were both familiar with the small 4-6-0s built for the Indian broad gauge, and probably with the similar engines of similar weight built for the Cape Government Railways, though the gauge there was 3' 6" as against the 5' 6" in India. In fact the first engines of the Cape 6th class were built by Dubs just when the Jones Goods were being built by Sharp, Stewart. The Highland engines were closely similar, but some ten tons heavier. Later a version with mixed traffic sized wheels appeared as the Highland 'Castle' class.

In 1903 James Manson produced the first of his 4-6-0 express locomotives for the Glasgow & South Western. These strikingly elegant machines differed substantially from the Highland ones. Their cylinders were still outside, but the valves were on top, and they had Belpaire fireboxes. Their appearances paralleled that of the first of the well known Indian Mail 4-6-0s, which resembled them greatly, and which were eventually built in large numbers over nearly half a century (and many of which are still at work to-day). By contrast, the Caledonian 4-6-0s with inside cylinders, last and largest examples of that earlier Scottish tradition, represented the end of a line rather than the beginning.

The new Scottish school came to England with R. W. Urie, and its final British expression was probably the Southern Railway 'King Arthur' class.

There was no specifically Scottish school of carriage design, though Hurst, Nelson of Motherwell built carriages for England as well as Scotland, but these were mostly of the familiar all-British type with rather low semi elliptical roofs and much recessed panelling along the sides. Only a close look could have differentiated North British from Glasgow & South Western, from Midland, Great Central, or L.S.W.R., if it were not for the colours. Such peculiarities as there were are referred to later.

Landscape and climate seemed to set the Scottish lines apart from those of England, if less apart from those of Wales. What one saw from the train was almost always beautiful, outside of the towns, and often highly dramatic. The lovely loneliness of the West Highland was, and is, unmatched for poetry in the British Isles, partly because the effect is sustained so long. And there is no finer seaside ride than the cliff top route between Berwick and Edinburgh, again a protracted pleasure and one heightened, for the northbound traveller, by the realisation that the Border has been crossed and by the altered tempo of impending arrival. Many long mileages of single track, especially towards the north of Scotland, enhance the sense of wildness and remoteness: on neither side of the train can the traveller see the way back, and no passing trains in the other direction can reassure that the train is not totally alone. On a slow rural branch line and on a short journey, single track arouses no special feelings, except perhaps those of getting closer to nature. But in a longer train, at a higher speed, for a couple of hours or more, the effect is really one of adventure.

The climate can be appalling, at any time of year, but it is in hard winters that all the Scottish railways make demands upon their operating staff seldom matched in England. Even the Glasgow & South Western, in what is reputed to be one of the mildest corners of the country, would have trains snowed up every hard winter, and that could, and can, be a bad business. Battling through a blizzard, finding the rails through thicker and thicker snow and building up a higher and higher wall in front of the engine, sometimes setting back and charging the obstacle, the train would finally come to a stand in some drifted cutting, with its driving wheels turning uselessly as they lifted on hard packed snow and lost contact with the rails. If the train was steam heated it might not be too bad for the passengers—for a time. But if it wasn't, they probably would crowd onto the locomotive footplate (there were often few travellers on these snowbound trains). There, the fire would be kept burning for as long as the fuel lasted and as long as there was water in the tender to keep the boiler full. But steam was being used the whole time, if not to heat the train, then at least to work the locomotive's blower to keep the fire alight. And the moment often came when the fire had to be thrown out, to save the boiler from exploding for lack of water, and after that all had to sit huddled in the train and wait for rescue. Exactly the same can happen to-day with diesel power: once the fuel runs out there is no heat or light, no power for anything. And even on electrified lines the snow can cause a power failure, or bring the wires down. Of course, the train dies long after everything has ceased to move on the roads, and when rescue comes eventually it comes by rail, with snowploughs.

The travellers on Scottish trains behave differently from those in English ones. Leaving aside urban commuters and football drunks, who are much the same all over Britain, one's companion on a Scottish train is more communicative, without actually being friendly. There seems to be recognition that it is quite ridiculous to sit opposite a stranger for an hour or two without some communication, and polite intercourse without the liberty of overfriendliness is natural. So it is that wonderful landscapes pass the window to the accompaniment of religious discussion, and politics punctuate the prospect of rivers, docks, and industrial sprawl. Food and drink and the niceties of their preparation are another likely topic, and sport of some kind is inescapable. And in Southern Scotland it is difficult to travel without being made aware of the discreet rivalry between Edinburgh and Glasgow. Perhaps the nicest thing about these conversations is the polite leave taking at the end of them, which leaves the feeling that the brief companionship has enhanced one's day.

So far nothing has been said of the beauty of trains in Scotland. To the writer, a railway track is often an enhancement of the landscape, unobtrusively delineating the curve of a hill or opening a fine avenue in a wood. It neither abuses and ignores the landscape, as a major road does, imposing a crude slash across it; nor does it conform totally, like a minor road, twisting round one field after another in an apparently random line, but still conspicuously differentiated in colour from its surroundings. The railway track is usually inconspicuous in colour and, in the open country, pursues a line which is a polite compromise with the landscape, requiring some earthworks and bridges, but suggestive of a courteous purposefulness. Scotland provides many perfect settings for railway tracks, and the very perfection of the setting enhances the beauty of the train passing through it. As a rule, Scottish trains were neat and seemly rather than conspicuously beautiful, but the Caledonian Railway made a bold and successful bid for a striking elegance in such trains as the 'Grampian corridor express' which was originally worked by the two 4-6-0s, Nos. 49 and 50, the lines of which were carefully studied to convey the maximum of style and size, and the royal blue livery of which was the perfect precursor of the long cream and maroon twelve-wheeled coaches of the train. Caledonian elegance was expressed in humbler trains than this, but elegance was by no means an exclusive Caledonian prerogative. There was no better looking locomotive in Scotland than a Manson 4-6-0 of the Glasgow & South Western and, as these locomotives worked the Midland trains from London north of Carlisle, the resplendent Midland coachwork, in its crimson livery, was again a splendid accompaniment to the locomotive. No Scottish locomotive was more impressive than a North British Atlantic, and, if the coaches behind it were sometimes somewhat box-like, the powerful personality of the high boilered locomotive yet provided an impressive spectacle. Further north, the trains of the Highland Railway were perhaps endearing rather than stylish, but the small locomotives of the Great North of Scotland always appeared beautifully proportioned at the heads of their two-tone trains. The flavour of all this was distinctly different from that of the great railways of England. The 'purple brown and spilt milk' carriages of the London & North Western, which looked so formal behind a shiny black L.N.W.R. locomotive, acquired a quality of more relaxed luxury when hauled by Caledonian blue. There was nothing in Scotland remotely like a rakish Great Western 'Saint', bustling along with its train of bulging-sided 70 footers, nor was there anything like an Ivatt Atlantic, with its austere outline, at the head of Great Northern varnished teak. Indeed, one senior officer of the Caledonian Railway once described the Ivatt Atlantics as 'fashionless' locomotives—what he would have said about some of the machines that ran in Austria passes the imagination. But it is worth recording that one Austrian engineer when shown a photograph of that epitome of the locomotive aesthetic, the Caledonian single driver No. 123, pointed in derision at the large splasher and said, 'Why do you prudish British conceal so much of those beautiful wheels?'.

The Scottish railways, then, had a distinctive character, setting, and custom. The freight traffic was not all fish, whisky, cattle, coal, and heavy machinery, but all these things, and especially the fish, were prominent in the railway scene. One last point, before coming to the specific railway companies, may be made, and that is that, to the traveller from England, the approach to Scotland invariably entailed some glimpses, at the very least, of the locomotives of the North British Railway. Very many of these bore names derived from the novels of Sir Walter Scott and others bore names relating to Scottish history and traditions. Even in comparatively recent years, arrival at the Border could be signalled by the sight of a locomotive bearing such a name as 'Laird o'Monkbarns', 'Thane of Fife', 'Baillie MacWheeble', and even 'Jingling Geordie'. There was no mistaking the fact that one was arriving in a different country.

The North British Railway

Major routes of the North British Railway

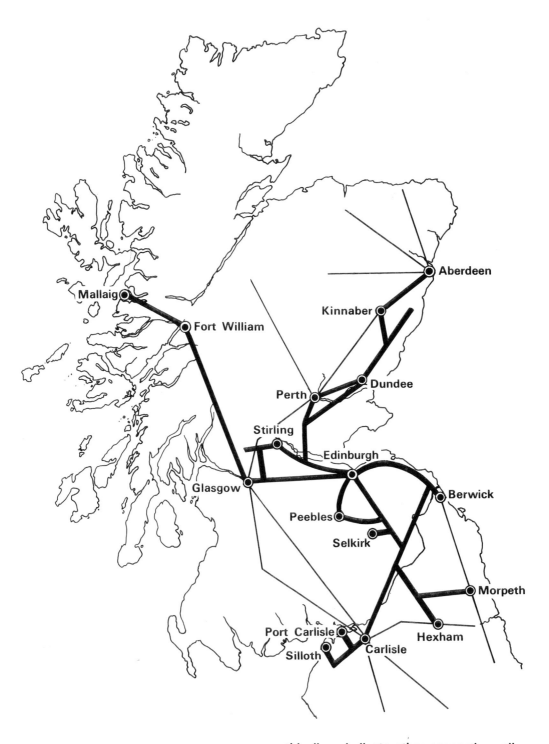

thin lines indicate other connecting railways

The North British Railway

1 The ultimate North British train with Atlantic 'The Lord Provost' at Inverkeithing

The North British Railway owed its name to the line between Berwick and Edinburgh. Eventually, this railway was to be the largest of all the Scottish companies, with a route mileage approaching 1,400, and thereby some 300 miles greater than the illustrious Caledonian. But, although it was larger than the Caledonian, it was certainly not more prosperous and its image was never quite as opulent as that of its western rival. However, the North British absorbed the Edinburgh & Glasgow Railway, which had the shortest route between the two principal cities of Scotland, and the direct connection that this afforded to Glasgow from the east coast main line was to prove an important asset.

The North British was made up of a large number of small Scottish companies and included in its constituents the oldest Scottish railway, the Monkland & Kirkintilloch. Although there were earlier railways of a purely industrial kind, as was only to be expected in an area of coal fields and iron works, the Monkland & Kirkintilloch was the first Scottish railway to be recognisably a public one, and therefore comparable with the Stockton & Darlington. As a result of the absorption of many small enterprises, details of which are given later, the North British eventually found itself with an extensive route mileage in southern Scotland. First and foremost, it ran from Berwick to Edinburgh, thereby continuing the east coast main line from London, at least after the completion of the Royal Border bridge at Berwick in 1850. Secondly, it had the best route between Edinburgh and

Glasgow, though its final Glasgow terminus at Queen Street lay at the foot of a formidable incline which required cable assistance to trains until the end of the first decade of the twentieth century. At the summit of this incline was Cowlairs, which was also the site of the main engineering works of the Company, where many locomotives were built, as well as carriages and other necessary parts for the railway. In the early twentieth century, the North British extended its tentacles from Glasgow to the west coast by building the West Highland Railway to Fort William, and eventually to Mallaig, the westernmost railway station in Britain. On the east side of the country it ran north from Edinburgh to Dundee and provided a network of lines in Fife, but these were connected to the main system by a train ferry across the Forth. This train ferry, the brainchild of Thomas Bouch, was in fact the first train ferry in the world, but it only provided continuous railway transportation for freight. Passengers had to de-train to cross the Forth. Another main line ran to Perth and, after the bridging of the estuary of the Tay, North British trains reached Aberdeen. The first Tay Bridge was, as is well known, destroyed in a gale in 1879. Its successor ensured the continuity of the east coast main line as far as Kinnaber Junction from which point North British trains reached Aberdeen by the exercise of running powers over the Caledonian Railway.

Those familiar with railway history will recall that, in 1888, there was a celebrated race to Edinburgh in which the east coast main line, consisting of the Great Northern, North Eastern, and North British Railway were partners in rivalry with the west coast main line which was London & North Western as far as Carlisle, and Caledonian thence to Edinburgh. But, at the end of 1890, the great Forth Bridge was opened—one of the many eighth wonders of the world, and thereafter the way was open for the races to Aberdeen which took place in 1895, with the same rivals. The North British, unlike the Caledonian, was dependent on two major feats of civil engineering, the Forth and Tay Bridges, for the completion of its system.

Another main line of the North British, which has unfortunately disappeared except for a stub end, was the Waverley Route which ran south from Edinburgh to Carlisle. Traversing the Border Country, the association with Sir Walter Scott was inevitable and the naming of this route after one of Scott's novels was a piece of felicitous public relations. It gave the North British a foothold in Carlisle, which was turned to advantage as a base for the tapping of the potential of the coast of north west England, at Port Carlisle, and also at Silloth. As the North British also enjoyed a near monopoly of the seaports of south east Scotland, it will be seen that its lines extended from the Irish Sea to the North Sea and from England far into Scotland.

In considering the growth of this far-flung railway, it is worth recording that the union between England and Scotland, though long established was, in the early nineteenth century as now, not an entirely easy one. Politically, it may be said that no incursion of an English railway into Scotland would have been tolerated, but an incursion of a Scottish railway into England seemed perfectly natural. One is reminded of Dr. Johnson's remark that the noblest prospect in the eyes of a Scotsman was the road that took him to England. Unkind and unfair as this remark undoubtedly was, it yet enshrined an attitude which was fully expressed by the railway promoters of the early nineteenth century. So it was that the North British could extend substantially into England, while no English railway was allowed to reach beyond Carlisle or Berwick.

There was at one time a suggestion that only one railway link between England and Scotland was necessary, just as there was at one time a suggestion that only one railway was needed to the south of London. Economic realities implied that this railway should run from Carlisle to Glasgow, but political realities dictated that the capital city, Edinburgh, could not take second place. So it was that eventually there were two main routes between Carlisle and Glasgow, and also two main routes between Carlisle and Edinburgh, and yet another, scarcely less important, main route on the east side of the country between Newcastle and Edinburgh and thence on to Glasgow. This last route was, of course, via Berwick, from which point the tracks were those of the North British Railway but it makes better economic sense to see this as a route from Newcastle.

The main lines of the North British Railway were, then, the east coast route to Edinburgh from Berwick, the Waverley route from Carlisle to Edinburgh, the Edinburgh & Glasgow Railway (to give it its pre-amalgamation title), Edinburgh to Dundee and Aberdeen, and to Perth. Scarcely less important from the point of view of revenue was an extensive network in south east Scotland and a substantial Glasgow suburban service out of which developed the West Highland main line to Fort William and Mallaig, the last being one of the most beautiful and dramatic railway lines in the whole of the British Isles.

It would be nice to record that so extensive an empire belonged to a prosperous railway company, but in practice the North British Railway was never as opulent as the Caledonian. Indeed, it had two periods in its history when it was decidedly parsimonous, partly from necessity but partly from inclination. Its carriages were never quite as long or quite as wide or quite as well-sprung as those of the Caledonian but this seems almost to have been a matter of philosophy rather than one of finance. The fact is that Edinburgh was the spiritual home of the North British and Glasgow the spiritual home of the Caledonian. Comparison between these two cities is very difficult, especially when the reader may have come from one or the other, but few will challenge the judgment that Edinburgh is the more frugal and rigorous minded. Glasgow, on the other hand, has historically been the city of vigorous industry and free thinking, notably lacking in inhibition. The suspicion has lingered in many minds that Caledonian prosperity was in the nature of a confidence trick and there can be little doubt that the frugal image of the North British was largely the product of the attitudes of one man, namely George Wieland, who was Chairman in the last years of the nineteenth century and the earlier years of the twentieth. Whatever the reason, the locomotives and rolling stock always presented the impression of being the minimum that would decently do the job, and it was not until after Wieland's death, that a distinct air of adventure and even prosperity began to settle over the railway.

The North British had more lines in England than its rival, and whether one approached Scotland by the east coast or the west coast route it was the locomotives and trains of the North British Railway that were most likely to herald the approach to the Border. That this should be so on the east coast was obvious, but to the traveller by the west coast route, arriving at Carlisle Citadel Station behind a London & North Western locomotive and expecting to be taken further by a Caledonian one, the immediate view of North British trains might suggest that the east coast route had been taken rather than the west. Carlisle Citadel Station presented the most fascinating and varied spectacle of any station in the days before Grouping. Here the black locomotives of the North Western were juxtaposed with the dark crimson of the Midland, the brown or, later, bronze green of the

2 Drummond's 2-2-2 express locomotive 'Berwick'

North British, the fine olive green of the Glasgow & South Western, or the blue of the Caledonian, while to the observant there was the added occasional glimpse of a train belonging to the Maryport & Carlisle. Of these three English and three Scottish railways, more is said in other chapters of this book and we are here only concerned with one of them, but the point made is that even the west coast traveller could be excused for believing that the N.B.R. was the most important, ubiquitous as it appeared to be in those towns close to the Border. On the other hand, trains from London via the East Coast mainline were taken right into Edinburgh by locomotives of the North Eastern Railway, apart from a short period when the N.B.R. was able to insist on an engine change at Berwick.

Whereas the route to Edinburgh from Berwick was not without its difficulties, that to Edinburgh from Carlisle was perhaps the most difficult major main line railway in the whole country. Considered in relation to its importance as a trunk route, it was certainly harder to work than even the Settle & Carlisle line of the Midland Railway. It was not only the gradients, though the summits at Whitrope and Falahill were approached by long gradients in both directions, but also there was a peculiarity about this and some other North British routes that all the stations of importance seemed to lie at the bottom of two gradients, so that it was not possible to use the momentum of the train to climb the hills in either direction. To make matters worse, it was firmly laid down, even in the last years before the Grouping that no locomotive could be used on express passenger work which had more than two coupled axles. It was this dictum propounded by the civil engineer Bell that resulted in the construction of the Atlantics. The Caledonian, Glasgow & South Western, and Highland Railways had all progressed to the 4-6-0, but the intense curvature of the North British main lines was seen as precluding this solution. In fact, the Atlantics were quite as effective as the overgrown 4-6-0s of the Caledonian. But it is one of the ironies of railway history that, in later years, Sir Nigel Gresley, probably the most imaginative and forward-looking of British twentieth century locomotive engineers, devised Britain's only eight coupled express locomotives especially for the North British main lines. Moreover, although, following the perverse tradition of permanent way engineers, Gresley's P.2s were sometimes accused of spreading the track, these engines were always recognised as being fully masters of any job ever presented to them on these difficult routes. And we must remember that the Atlantics were also accused of spreading the track in the first years of their existence.

3 An old Wheatley survivor into L.N.E.R. days

As an indication of the actual severity of the North British main lines, the main line between Edinburgh and Carlisle, known as the Waverley route, and now, alas, a thing of the past, contained the two summits already mentioned, the climbs to which, from both sides, were up gradients between 1 in 70 and 1 in 100, over distances of around 10 miles, complicated by curvature and often subject to high winds. The main line north from Edinburgh to Dundee had less formidable banks, but, again, the stations were all in the bottoms of the hollows of the gradient profile. The opening of the Forth Bridge at the end of 1890 added to the operating problems facing the locomotives and it was regular practice to provide pilot or banking assistance up to the Bridge from Inverkeithing and sometimes even from the Edinburgh side. Banking assistance was not normally required further north, though the work was still extremely hard, but it remained a fact for many years that trains from the south via Berwick could only reach Waverley Station unassisted if they were not stopped at signals a couple of miles outside. If they should be stopped banking assistance was usually needed to push them up that last short stretch through the tunnel into the Waverley Station which, incidentally, was the largest railway station in the British Isles outside of London.

The locomotive history of the Railway is notable for the fact that, in spite of the severity of the routes, there was never a six-coupled passenger locomotive, nor yet an eight-coupled freight one. But it was on the North British that the most typical express type associated with the British Isles first made its appearance. The 4-4-0 with inside cylinders and inside frames was first built by Thomas Wheatley in 1871, and it was one of these engines that fell with its train to the bottom of the River Tay on that stormy night in 1879 when the high girders of the first Tay Bridge collapsed. Though none of the 79 people on that train survived, the locomotive did and put in many more years of service. It even attained the unique distinction of conversion to a four cylinder tandem compound on Nesbit's system, one of only three tandem compounds ever to run in these islands, the other two being broad and standard gauge inside cylinder 2-4-0 engines of the Great Western Railway. The North British engine at least performed satisfactorily though not

4 One of Matthew Holmes' West Highland bogies, at Dunbar in later days. The tender cab is an addition

with sufficient distinction to justify the perpetuation of the design, whereas the Great Western examples were both catastrophic failures.

Wheatley's engines were characterised by inside cylinders and inside frames and a certain plainness of outline which was nevertheless admirably proportioned. Moreover, although he left under a cloud in 1874 (which had nothing to do with his technical ability), quite a number of his locomotives survived to be taken into the stock of the L.N.E.R. fifty years later. After two 4-4-0s he produced two 2-4-0s, followed by a further batch and six of these, more or less renewed or re-built, entered L.N.E.R. stock. In 1873 came four somewhat enlarged 4-4-0s. But it was Wheatley's 0-6-0 which was his most distinctive legacy. They first appeared in 1867, but no less than thirty-seven of them, half of the total built, were taken over by the L.N.E.R. Under Wheatley's guidance Cowlairs works was re-organised and became a main producer of locomotives for the railway.

Wheatley's successor was Dugald Drummond. Drummond was a disciple of William Stroudley, and was to spread that great designer's ideas and style over the North British and later the Caledonian, and even, through his influence upon his younger brother, Peter, over the Highland, if not the Glasgow & South Western. Stroudley had been works manager at Cowlairs, where the elder Drummond was a foreman, and Stroudley had gone as Locomotive Superintendent to the Highland before moving south to the London, Brighton & South Coast Railway. He was not a Scotsman but he aroused such powerful admiration and loyalty in the two Drummond brothers that Dugald followed him to Brighton and became his works manager, and Peter joined the team some time later.

Drummond was appointed in 1875 and the first thing he did was to produce a very slightly enlarged version of his master's 'Terrier' 0-6-0 tank. He introduced a few minor features of his own, such as the safety valves on top of the dome, but he also brought with him the Brighton practice of naming engines after the localities which they were serving, and the whole outline of the locomotives was unmistakeably Stroudley. Next came the 0-6-0 goods engine and two 2-2-2 express locomotives, again slight enlargements of their Brighton prototypes. These locomotives were named Glasgow and Berwick and worked the express services between these two towns including through carriages from

5 One of the small Reid goods engines recently returned from overseas service, in 1919, still bearing the unofficial name 'Joffre'

Kings Cross. They were excellent machines, but not suitable for other routes of the railway and so, when, in 1876, the Midland Railway's Settle & Carlisle line was about to be opened to traffic, and the North British had secured the right to conduct the Midland trains from Carlisle to Edinburgh, Drummond proceeded to a 4-4-0. The route over which these engines were required to pass was a very difficult one, as has already been explained, and was never conceived as a major through route. Something more powerful than the Wheatley 4-4-0s was required and in providing it, Drummond built the first locomotives which were more his own than Stroudley's, though much of their appearance still sugge-sted the Brighton connection. They had proper Adams type bogies and long sloping grates giving 21 sq. ft. of area. The cylinders were 18 ins. × 26 ins. with the valves between, and the coupled wheels were 6 ft. 6 ins. in diameter. These twelve engines were admirable in every way and were the true prototypes of many Scottish 4-4-0s on several railways.

Among the other locomotives designed by Drummond for the North British, there was a class of 0-4-2 tank engines clearly based on Stroudley's D class. The type was less suited to North British tracks and was re-built by Drummond with trailing bogies. It may be for this reason that, for his next batch of tank engines, he adopted the 4-4-0 wheel arrangement. There were three of these quite large locomotives with 6 ft. driving wheels and they were, in effect, a slightly reduced version of his 4-4-0 tender engines. They were a great success and for lighter duties Drummond produced a miniature version of which no less than thirty were built. Over the same period, more than one hundred enlarged 0-6-0s were added to stock. Drummond scarcely put a foot wrong and his work on the North British was of the highest class. It is not surprising that the Caledonian angled for his services and offered him sufficiently attractive terms to result in his transferring from Cowlairs to nearby St. Rollox in 1882.

6 Reid saturated 4-4-2 tank on Edinburgh suburban train

Drummond was only with the North British for seven years but his successor, Matthew Holmes remained three times as long before dying in harness. Holmes did not depart from the school of design which Drummond had established and had taken with him to the Caledonian Railway. Indeed, anything that the Caledonian did in the next twenty years, the North British did, but rather less lavishly. The two most obvious signs of this were that the North British tended to build locomotives in smaller numbers, that their livery was less resplendent, and the cabs provided for the enginemen less comfortable, at least until W. P. Reid succeeded Holmes in 1903. But, undoubtedly, they were fine machines. In the races to Aberdeen in 1895, when the recent opening of the Forth Bridge provoked a second outburst of rivalry between the east and west coast groups, the large Holmes 4–4–0s acquitted themselves with great distinction, though the staff at stations did not always enter into the spirit of the thing.

At the beginning of the twentieth century it was apparent to the travelling public and even to the Board of Directors that the North British Railway had fallen very far in public esteem below the Caledonian. There was nothing wrong in the locomotives themselves, they were indeed excellent if small, but they could only be used to work the heaviest trains over that difficult system because those trains were in fact not particularly heavy, being composed of rather lightweight and distinctly spartan carriages. When the luxurious Midland trains had to be hauled over the Waverley Route from Carlisle to Edinburgh, the engines frequently had to be used in pairs. There was nothing on the North British to compare in size and grandeur even with Manson's 4-6-0s on the Glasgow & South Western, let alone the Blue giants of the Caledonian. Fortunately, George Wieland, for many years the shrewd and parsimonious Chairman of the Company, left the scene and a more expansively minded Board was installed in time to face the challenge presented by the Caledonian 'Grampian Corridor Express' which made its debut in 1905 and was composed of twelve-wheeled carriages of great luxury and beauty.

The answer which eventually emerged was a new Aberdeen express train set, not quite the equal of the Caledonian one, but still very handsome, and the locomotive provided to

7 'Glen Douglas' as now restored. A Reid superheated 4-4-0 with smaller wheels for the West Highland line

haul it was the celebrated Atlantic. Whereas three of the five Scottish Railways had by this time adopted the 4-6-0 wheel arrangement, the North British civil engineer would not allow so extended a coupled wheel base. Reid actually designed a 4-6-0 and there was even talk of producing a large 4-4-0 three cylinder compound based on the Midland engines which were proving as capable as most 4-6-0s in Great Britain in this period, though, of course, they rather lacked adhesion weight. In the end Reid was allowed to build a ten-wheeled engine but it is perhaps fair to point out that the burly North British Atlantic, in spite of the (unjustified) claims of excessive fuel consumption and the (more justified) claims of rough riding, proved a better and longer lasting machine than any of the great Caledonian 4-6-0s.

Although none of these Atlantics has been preserved, their image is the hallmark of the railway to most people to-day, more so than that of the preserved 'intermediate' 4-4-0 'Glen Douglas'. The Atlantic was often photographed running through the massive girders of the Forth Bridge, and it was also the subject of a highly inaccurate but very popular commercial model. The only other Scottish locomotives to receive this particular accolade were Caledonian, but those commercial models were sponsored by the Caledonian Railway itself. The Atlantic deserved its fame because both its appearance and its perform-ance were very striking. It bore some resemblance to the greatly admired Atlantics of the Great Central, but the boilers and cylinders were much larger and the cab, rather like that of a North Eastern engine, was an elegant affair with two windows on each side. On the Aberdeen route with a heavy train, the work confronting the locomotive was such that the tender had to be piled as high as possible with coal, and North British firemen were especially skilled in the art of doing this safely. Even so, one of these trains often completed the round trip with an empty tender. The large outside cylinders inevitably led to some rough riding and, to those that have seen it, the sight of a North British Atlantic getting into its stride at the beginning of its journey was quite unforgettable, as the great engine lurched and swung, roaring from the chimeny, with its coal mountain rising behind the cab. The writer has to confess that he only saw this spectacle once, but he has never

8 Another angle of a North British Atlantic, magnificent from all angles. Note the tablet catcher on the tender

forgotten it. On that occasion, the engine was in the apple green of the L.N.E.R., which suited it to perfection. To judge from the surviving coloured illustrations of the engines in North British days, they looked very well in the rather elaborately lined out brown livery in which they first appeared, but the darkish green which was later adopted did not particularly flatter any locomotive and the biggest ones least of all.

W. P. Reid's other locomotives were mostly worthy enlargements of those of his predecessors. The distinctive commodious cab with a single side window somewhat forward of the central position was better, for once, than was ever provided on the Caledonian Railway, if we except the very small group of Caledonian 4-6-0s which received side window cabs, just at the end of J. F. McIntosh's time. With these comfortable cabs, the North British locomotives again began to receive names. The large superheated 'intermediate' 4-4-0s received the names of Scottish glens, while their larger-wheeled equivalent express locomotives received those of the characters of the novels of Sir Walter Scott. Superheating came in Reid's time and further improved what were already very sound locomotives.

With one conspicuous exception, then, the locomotive stock was composed of sound and seemly locomotives distinguished mainly by their orthodoxy. In addition to the 4-4-0s there were of course equivalent 0-6-0 goods engines, and there were 0-4-4 and 4-4-2 tanks, 0-6-0 and 0-6-2 tanks, the latter originally built for banking trains up the incline from the Glasgow terminus at Queen Street. All of Reid's engines, many of Holmes', some of Drummond's and even Wheatley's served the L.N.E.R. well, and most of Reid's engines lasted well into the last few years of steam, the big 0-6-0s being among the very last survivors.

The coaching stock was long painted dark red so that it almost matched that of the Midland Railway or the North Eastern, with which it was frequently juxtaposed. But, because the L.N.E.R. somehow managed to preserve the individuality of its pre-grouping constituents, an Atlantic and train in L.N.E.R. colours was still essentially North British. The light green paint on the engine, and the brown paint on the carriages did little to detract from this aspect. It was one of the pleasures of observing the railways of Britain in the thirties and forties to recognise the pre-grouping origin of the almost uniformly painted coaching and wagon stock, and, though the wood panelled N.B.R. stock lost something by its change of hue, the steel panelled coaches of the Railway's last years looked just as well in brown as in the dark green which had rather unfortunately been adopted in the last independent years.

The foregoing will perhaps have conveyed the message that, in the end, the railway had provided itself with some excellent locomotives and some handsome rolling stock. Much of this lasted well into the years of nationalisation, but, unhappily, the Atlantics themselves, the symbols of revival, did not. They were too large and powerful to be used economically on secondary duties and so after some thirty years, when their place was taken by Gresley Pacifics and 2-8-2s, they were withdrawn over a comparatively short span of time, as their boilers came up for renewal. One of them, 'Midlothian', was in fact designated for preservation and, when this happened, Gresley's instructions reached Scotland almost too late. The locomotive was already in pieces, some of which had been cut up, but there were enough components lying around to make it possible to restore the engine and return it to service. After a brief Indian summer, which extended into the early months of the War, it was quietly withdrawn and cut up at a time when national preservation loomed larger than locomotive preservation.

Although this was to become the largest railway in Scotland in terms of route mileage, its beginnings were modest. In 1844, the North British Railway Act was sanctioned, authorising a line 57½ miles long from Edinburgh via Dunbar and Burnmouth to Berwick. This line was opened in 1846 with 5 main line trains daily in each direction and an early morning market train from Berwick soon to become a regular feature of the line. Several feeder lines were constructed to the main route including in 1849, the Roston-Duns line and the short branch to Tranent pits near Prestonpans.

The N.B.R.'s attempt to reach Carlisle began in 1845 with the authorisation of the Edinburgh & Hawick Railway, planned to serve the industries of the important tweed producing towns. The line ran from the Edinburgh & Dalkeith Railway at Dalhousie via Gorebridge, Tynehead and Melrose and was incorporated in the N.B.R. soon after its authorisation. To complete the route, the N.B.R. bought the Edinburgh and Dalkeith line which had been opened in 1831. The coming of the railway had a very beneficial effect on the tweed industry in the area and was a considerable boon to the livestock trade of St. Boswells and Hawick. Branch lines were built to Kelso in 1850–1, to Selkirk in 1856 and to Jedburgh in 1860, the Kelso line linking with the York, Newcastle & Berwick branch line in England. In 1866 a loop line was constructed from Eskbank on the Edinburgh & Hawick line via Roslin, Peebles and Cardonna to Galashiels, and this was to play an important role in the development of Peebles as a spa holiday resort in the 1880s. The real goal of the Edinburgh & Hawick line remained Carlisle but there was tough competition from the Caledonian to reach the town. After a hard battle against a rival Caledonian

When you
VISIT SCOTLAND

Anticipation.

Travel by the
North British
Railway.

THE LINE

FOR

SPEED & COMFORT.

You must see :

THE LAND OF SCOTT—Melrose and Dryburgh Abbeys, Abbotsford House, &c.

THE LAND OF WALLACE AND BRUCE Dunfermline Abbey, Stirling Castle, &c.

ROB ROY'S COUNTRY—Loch Katrine, Trossachs, Loch Lomond, &c.

PRINCE CHARLIE'S COUNTRY Fort William (for Ben Nevis), Glenfinnan (for Loch Shiel), Mallaig, &c.

THE FIRTH OF CLYDE SUMMER RESORTS—Dunoon, Rothesay, &c. (*via* Craigendoran).

THE HADDINGTONSHIRE AND FIFESHIRE GOLFING RESORTS—North Berwick, Gullane, &c.; St. Andrews, Lundin Links, &c.

About 200 Golf Courses to choose from.

ASK FOR TICKETS via East Coast or Midland Route, thence North British Railway.

A Post Card to Mr. J. Black, Superintendent of the Line, Edinburgh, will bring a Guide Book and all particulars.

The North British Railway Company's Hotels adjoin the Stations at—

EDINBURGH (Waverley). Telegrams : " British, Edinburgh."
GLASGOW (Queen Street). Telegrams : " Attractive, Glasgow."
PERTH (General Station). Telegrams : " Station Hotel, Perth."

Edinburgh. *W. F. JACKSON, General Manager.*

9 North British publicity, 1914

proposal, the N.B.R. gained the right to build the Border Union Railway between Carlisle and Hawick. The line, with branches to Langholm and Gretna, was opened in 1862, but that was by no means the end of the N.B.R.'s difficulties; for the Caledonian, in conjunction with the L.N.W.R., placed an embargo on traffic travelling to Edinburgh via the N.B.R. unless specifically marked. The operation was so successful that the N.B.R. had to find an alternative route from the south. This it did by leasing and then absorbing the Carlisle & Silloth Bay Railway & Docks Company so that any goods from the south could be loaded onto N.B.R. trains at Silloth Bay and taken through to Edinburgh untouched by the C.R. or the L.N.W.R. at Carlisle.

Concurrently with the Border Union Railway another major link with England was being established at Hexham, with the opening of the Border Counties Railway from Riccarton. Richard Hodgson, chairman of the N.B.R., had agreed to help the line financially and it soon came under his direction. The following year (1863) the N.B.R. acquired an extension to the Border Counties line in the Wansbeck Valley Railway, opened in stages between Reedsmouth and Morpeth. Further north, in 1862 the N.B.R. absorbed the West of Fife Railway & Harbour Company and the Edinburgh, Perth & Dundee Railway to establish a virtual monopoly of the coastline between the river Tweed and the Tay and this was followed in 1865 by the absorption of the famous Edinburgh & Glasgow Railway, itself a combination of the Glasgow, Dumbarton & Helensburgh and the Caledonian & Dumbarton lines.

The next great step was to build two giant bridges across the Firths of Forth and Tay. The Act for the Tay bridge was passed in 1870 and Thomas Bouch appointed designer. There were many problems in erecting the 2 mile, 85 span, bridge, not least of which was the shoddy workmanship of the Wormit ironfoundry; but all defects, however serious, were successfully 'covered up' and in 1878 the bridge was inspected by the Board of Trade and opened for public use. One and a half years later, in December 1879, it collapsed in a fierce gale, pitching the 5.20 p.m. train from Burntisland to Dundee into the Tay, killing all 79 passengers. Bouch was ruined and all his plans for the Forth bridge, approved in 1873, were abandoned. There was inevitably some delay before work could continue on bridging the Forth and the Tay, but Bouch's bridge had at least demonstrated the immense advantages of having a direct link across the Firths. Construction work was beginning on the new Forth Bridge designed by John Fowler and Benjamin Baker, to consist of 6 cantilevers mounted in pairs on 3 towers. The main contract was signed in 1882 and the bridge opened by the Marchioness of Tweeddale and the Prince of Wales in 1890. As a result of the opening of the bridge and its associated approach lines, the distance between Edinburgh and Aberdeen was cut to 130 miles by the N.B.R. against 159 by the Caledonian, and the distance between Edinburgh and Perth cut to 48 miles by the N.B.R. against 69 by the C.R.

In Edinburgh itself, the volume of traffic entering the company's station at Waverley increased substantially, necessitating considerable enlargements. The work began in 1892 and upon completion Waverley had become the largest station in the country with 18 acres of passenger accommodation and 5 acres for goods.

By the turn of the century, the North British had become a railway noted for speed on its main lines, playing its own important part in running the East Coast express trains from London. During the 1888 races to Edinburgh, the North Eastern had done all the running,

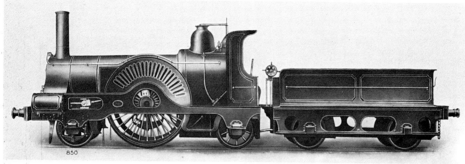

10 Caledonian Primitive: a modified Crewe 2-2-2

but in 1895 it was left to the Matthew Holmes 6 ft. 6 ins. engines to complete the race from Edinburgh to Aberdeen. This was the normal pattern of running, with the N.E.R. heading the trains to Edinburgh and the N.B.R. thence to Kinnaber Junction and Aberdeen, until 1897. Then the N.B.R. ousted the North Eastern and insisted on providing engines for all the East Coast trains north of Berwick. In spite of having to change engines at Berwick, the North British managed to maintain the swift schedules established by the N.E.R. to Edinburgh, sometimes clocking speeds of 80 m.p.h. The report of the Railway Commission in 1898 however, ended the brief spell of N.B.R. traction by deciding in favour of the North Eastern, and once again N.E.R. locomotives were to be seen hauling the East Coast trains into Edinburgh.

Within Scotland itself, the North British had built up a considerable traffic between Edinburgh and the West coast, and a thriving holiday business to East coast resorts such as Eyemouth and North Berwick, developed by the railway into a first class golfing centre. The company also ran steamers from Silloth to Dublin and from the Clyde to Lochgoilhead, Dunoon and Arrochar. Along the Clyde and in Glasgow itself, congestion had severely affected the North British until 1886, when the Glasgow, City & District Railway was built under Glasgow to link the east with the west of the city and provide a through route from Edinburgh to the West coast.

The North British was one of Scotland's big dock owners, laying claim to docks at Burntisland, Methil, Silloth, Bo'ness and Alloa. Burntisland docks, opened in 1896, were the largest under N.B.R. control, by 1910 comprising 43¼ acres. Coal, fish and market produce were the mainstay of the line and by 1910 the company was carrying 22 million tons of minerals and 5 million tons of merchandise.

Perhaps the most scenic route on the N.B.R. was that to Mallaig in the Western Highlands. Inverness, the Highland capital, was jealously guarded by the Highland Railway, and although the N.B.R. did manage to reach Fort Augustus on the route there it dared venture no further. Other areas however were open to development and the opportunity for expansion came with the promotion of the West Highland Railway, authorised in 1889 to construct a line from Craigendoran to Fort William and later a branch to Banavie. Opened in 1894, the line was worked by the N.B.R. until its complete absorption in 1908. During that time the Mallaig branch, terminating at the sound of Sleat and offering rail connections for the Stornaway and Portree steamers had been built and opened. Passing through mountainous countryside and running down to the coast by Lochailort, the Mallaig branch offered views scarcely to be matched in this country. Right up to 1923 the West Highland managed to retain a certain individuality, with the N.B.R. building special locomotives and carriages for the route. Perhaps the best known was the 'West Highland Coupe Composite Brake Carriage' built in 1895 with one and a half 1st class compartments, and two and a half 3rd class, at opposite ends of the carriage, each end coupe having observation windows.

The general standard of accommodation on the N.B.R., however, was not always so high. In the 1850s and 60s the carriages had been of the 4 wheeled box type, many bought from outside contractors, but in 1867 Cowlairs became the principal locomotive works of the company and all new construction was to be done there. One of the great triumphs of Cowlairs was undoubtedly the production, in 1873, of the first sleeping carriage for use on the East Coast line from Kings Cross, almost a year before the introduction of a similar carriage on the West Coast. During the 1880s most of the main line stock consisted of 35½ ft. 6 wheeled composite carriages with two 1st class and two 3rd class compartments. Bogie coaches were not introduced until well into the 1890s.

In common with most other lines, the stock found on the local lines left much to be desired, while very superior coaches appeared where competition was keenest, as for instance, when in 1905–6, to compete with the Caledonian's Aberdeen service, the N.B.R. produced block trains of 57 ft. 8 in. coaches. The best Edinburgh to Aberdeen trains consisted of two 3rd class, a composite, a composite diner and a luggage brake. Even the suburban stock around Edinburgh and Glasgow improved considerably towards the last years, with 8 wheeled coaches in block sets running on most trains.

The war told heavily on the N.B.R., and its locomotives and rolling stock suffered considerably from intensive use in carrying naval traffic to and from Invergordon and Scapa. The situation was so bad that following the restoration of peace, William Whitelaw, chairman of the company, felt in duty bound to fight and eventually win a long hard legal battle with the government over its compensation payments. The company was finally awarded £9,790,545, and on the formation of the L.N.E.R., William Whitelaw, with an enhanced reputation, was elected chairman of the new group.

By 1923 it could not be said that the North British had an outstanding reputation as an efficient and comfortable railway. Nevertheless, it had undoubtedly contributed greatly to the life and development of Scotland, serving Clydeside and the coalfields of Monkland, Lothian and Fife, and it could lay claim to two monumental engineering feats in the Forth and Tay bridges. It had introduced the first sleeping carriage to be used in this country and was the only Scottish railway to adopt centralised traffic control to any notable extent. It might not have been the most luxurious railway in Scotland but no-one could deny that, in its own way, the North British had held the Border against the Sassenachs: it remained essentially Scottish in character.

Major Routes of the Caledonian Railway

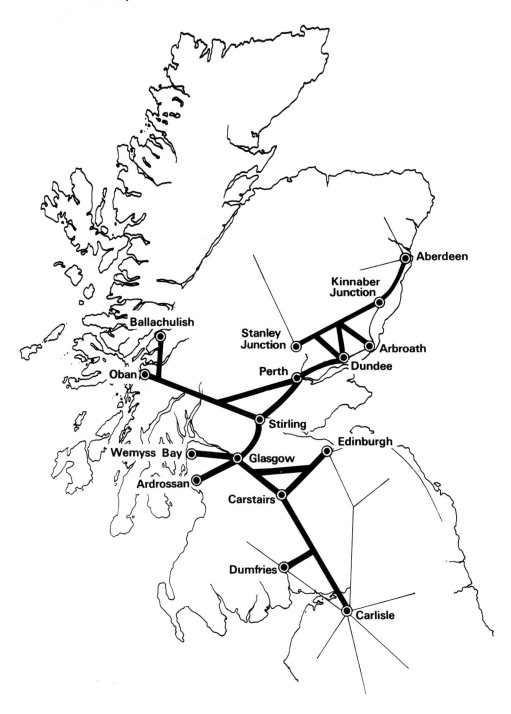

thin lines indicate other connecting railways

The Caledonian Railway

11 Caledonian Renaissance: one of Benjamin Conner's express 2-4-0s

The Caledonian was a great railway. The great are not always good, but they always bear the stamp of their greatness and for many reasons which are hard to define, the Caledonian had an air of confidence and authority which expressed itself in the design of its loco-motives, carriages, and principal stations.

This was not the largest Scottish railway though it was the most powerful and pros-perous. It owed its position to its partnership with the London & North Western in the west coast route from London to Scotland. The London & North Western was another 'great' railway and though it did many things badly it did some things supremely well and served a particularly prosperous industrial area which in turn served the growth and prosperity of the railway. It was inevitable that the extension of this route north of the border to Glasgow and, less importantly, to Edinburgh, would confer greatness on the northern partner.

The Caledonian was in fact slightly later in its origins than the North British but it was able to secure the right to build over the most direct route between Carlisle and Glasgow. Its eventual absorption of the Scottish Central Railway took it via Perth to Aberdeen, with connections to Inverness over the tracks of the Highland Railway. It was thus possible in the later nineteenth century and after to take a sleeping car from Euston Station in London right through to Inverness. This attracted a wealthy clientele of sportsmen who would travel north with their guns, luggage, servants and dogs in large numbers at certain times of the year and thereby provide a useful revenue for all three railways but, perhaps more

12 One of the only numerous British class of outside cylindered, long boiler goods engines

importantly, reinforce the social status of these lines and provide them with an opportunity of advertising their efficiency to some of the most influential and wealthy persons in the land.

As far as the Caledonian share was concerned, it was always obvious that enormous attention was paid to the appearance of the locomotives which took over the luxurious trains at Carlisle. These trains were made up of carriages which were, for the most part, jointly owned and known as the West Coast Joint Stock. The Caledonian was unwilling to juxtapose anything much inferior which might have sufficed for purely internal services, so the example of the great trains stimulated Caledonian carriage designers to maintain a very high standard on purely Scottish routes. The culmination of this policy was the superb 'Grampian Corridor Express' of 1905.

Although the great period of the Caledonian, as of most British railways, was in the late nineteenth and early twentieth centuries, the line was already showing signs of a dashing personality in the 1850s. The locomotive engineer until 1856 was Robert Sinclair who later went to the Great Eastern. Sinclair was a figure of European importance and his designs for the Caledonian appeared virually unchanged on various European lines. He seems to have been the first to use the 2-4-2 wheel arrangement in a tender locomotive. This was an extension of the Stephenson long boiler design, with outside cylinders, but to the basic 2-4-0 configuration, having all the axles under the boiler barrel, he added trailing wheels behind the firebox which made it possible to enlarge this part of the locomotive and at the same time to stablise its running. Sinclair's first essay in the type appeared on the Grand Luxemburg Railway but this was an important first, because 2-4-2 express engines eventually became very numerous in Europe and especially in France where they eventually evolved into the Atlantic type with the introduction of a leading bogie. The Caledonian thus started its life with a locomotive engineer of high standing and maintained this quality right through to the outbreak of the First World War.

The growth of the system and the various political triumphs associated with it are recounted later. We are here mainly concerned with the character of this railway as it showed itself in the years of its greatness and which was very well expressed in its very title. The name Caledonian was so unspecific, so all-embracing, that it clearly conveyed the impression that this railway belonged to all of Scotland, or that all of Scotland belonged to it, whereas the others were decidedly provincial by comparison. Lordliness was further expressed in its choice of colour schemes. The coaching stock was painted in a style barely distinguishable from that of the London & North Western – in itself striking enough. The locomotives were blue: at first a dark, royal, blue, and in later years almost a sky blue, but whatever the shade it was bolder than the discreet green of the Highland or the 'Sou' West', the bright green of the G.N.S. or the sober brown or bronze-green of the North British. Over the years the Caledonian colour proceeded from the Royal to the heavenly.

The Caledonian was fiercely territorial and, although Glasgow was by no means its exclusive preserve, the fact that it provided the shortest and most luxurious connection from London to that city made it exceedingly jealous of the incursions of others. In fact, it was very far from enjoying a monopoly of the Glasgow area services. Both the Glasgow & South Western and the North British were largely in evidence and in much of the Glasgow area the competition was extremely fierce. Generally speaking, the Caledonian had rather less of the local traffic than the 'Sou' West'. But, as always, the Caledonian contrived to spread an aura of opulence over the routes which it did serve. For the Clyde Coast services it provided fully fledged express locomotives, luxurious stock, and steamers which, though not always the fastest, were always the most luxurious on the Estuary. Inland it ran such phenomena as the 'Tinto Express' which was essentially a superior kind of commuter train which ran fast between Glasgow and Thankerton and then stopped at a series of country stations on which it conferred the questionable status of remoter dormitories. This train even included a Pullman car.

Pullman cars and named trains were a speciality of the Caledonian and at one time it had more named trains than any other British railway. It was the only Scottish railway to run Pullman cars on a large scale, and one of these was a unique observation car with a completely glazed end, for which reason it had to be marshalled at the rear of the train. This famous vehicle was named 'Maid of Morven' and was perhaps a forerunner of the 'Beavertail' observation cars which were fitted to L.N.E.R. streamlined expresses between the Wars.

As with so many of the pre-grouping railways, the great period ran from the 1880s to 1914. Previously, the Caledonian by no means presented the same image of unassailable confidence. All the railways in Scotland had a struggle to make ends meet, because Scotland was and is more thinly populated than the southern parts of the British Isles and there simply was not the volume of traffic, passenger or goods, to justify expensive capital investment. But the Caledonian contrived, in the 1880s, to lift itself as no other Scottish railway quite did. Exactly how it did this cannot easily be analysed, but it must be remembered that a great deal of English capital went in to railways in southern Scotland and the boards of directors, while carefully arranging not to offend the patriotism of the Scots, yet contained many English financiers. There can be no doubt that it was the enlargement of the ambitions of the London & North Western Railway which brought prosperity to the Caledonian. The English company had not been particularly interested in its northern route to Carlisle when Manchester and Liverpool and their surrounding industrial towns had been such a lucrative source of revenue. But the growing importance of Glasgow in the industrial scene in the middle of the 19th century attracted the attentions of the directors of the L.N.W.R. and their ambitions raised the Caledonian to its eventual eminence and prosperity. Thus it was that a frugally operated and economically built railway (though possessed of some of the best routes) was enabled to expand.

A fair symptom of what was taking place was the offer which enticed Dugald Drummond from the North British to the Caledonian in 1882. Drummond had done excellent work for his previous employers and his standing in engineering circles was high. His base was already in Glasgow, the North British works being at Cowlairs, and it is said that the tempting offer came from a director of the Caledonian over lunch. An individual appointment does not change the fortunes of a railway company but it may be symptomatic of them, and certainly Drummond was an eminently worthwhile acquisition.

Before 1882, the locomotive stock of the Caledonian Railway was characterised by outside cylinders. It was the only British railway which had made extensive use of the outside cylinder, long boiler 0-6-0 which was once so ubiquitous on the European mainland. The passenger locomotives had long been predominantly of the 2-4-0 wheel arrangement, and some of these had been excellent machines, notably those built to the designs of Benjamin Conner. There were still locomotives which could be attributed to Alexander Allan, one time works manager at Crewe and later in charge of the locomotive affairs of the Scottish Central Railway which was taken over by the Caledonian in 1865. Allan's influence in Scotland is referred to in more detail in the chapter on the Highland Railway. Here it is only necessary to point out that it was a surprise to some that this well-known engineer did not become the superintendent of the Caledonian, but Conner may well have been the more able engineer. His designs reflected an earlier close association with Allan and versions of the 'Crewe type' were once as common on the Caledonian as on the Highland. Conner's masterpiece was probably the 8 ft. single driver express locomotive which had very large cylinder ports and valves and was a notably free running machine. These engines later were the subject of some modifications by Drummond which did not improve them but, on the other hand, he did successfully enlarge some of Conner's mixed traffic 2-4-0s, and thereby ensured that these delightful locomotives remained long in evidence on the system. There were also many 0-4-2 tender locomotives, also with outside cylinders, which were used primarily for goods traffic, and there were even outside cylinder 2-4-2 tanks. George Brittain had succeeded, in 1876, and had introduced the 4-4-0 type to passenger service but he resigned after six years owing to ill health.

There is no doubt that Drummond did an excellent job at St. Rollox, as he had done at Cowlairs. He was tempted away after 1882 by a splendid offer which came to nothing and tried his hand at independent locomotive manufacturing but he eventually succeeded William Adams on the London & South Western. There is perhaps something to be learned of Drummond's character in the restlessness with which he pursued his career. With equal restlessness he pursued improvements in the design of the steam locomotive and he probably did his best work on the Caledonian. Excellent though his earlier locomotives were, the Caledonian ones were better and when he went to the south of England his judgement clearly began to fade. It may well be that he found the pastoral L.S.W.R., fast though some of its services were, rather a backwater after the northern portion of the West Coast main line.

Apart from the modernisation of old engines which Drummond pursued with a very large measure of success and the rationalisation of the railway workshops, which was always close to his heart and which was later to be his greatest contribution to the

13 Mystery picture: a McIntosh mixed traffic 0-6-0 rouses the echoes as it leaves old Glasgow Central, with two 12 wheeled L.N.W.R. coaches in its train and garlands on its boiler. The circumstances are not known

L.S.W.R., Drummond produced four basic designs for the Caledonian. They were an express 4-4-0, a smaller wheeled version for the Clyde Coast services, a standard 6 coupled goods and a 0-4-4 suburban tank. All of these had inside cylinders. Attention inevitably centres on the express locomotives, because the nature of their work required the greatest staying effort and within this series there were some variations. Originally, the standard Drummond cylinder block copied the practice of his master, Stroudley, in having the valves between the cylinders and the ports divided, the lower exhaust port connecting with the blast pipe via a duct taken right round the cylinder. This arrangement made the locomotives freer-running than most having valves between the cylinder bores. The idea was extended further in four of the engines, which also had the high boiler pressure, for the period, of 200 p.s.i. In these four locomotives the ports were not only divided, with upper and lower portions, but they were moved to the cylinder ends, each end having its own exhaust port. The idea was to make the passages as direct as possible

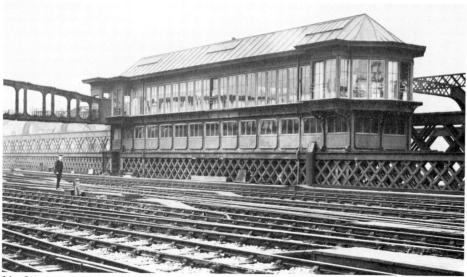

14 Caledonian architecture: 1) Glasgow Central Signal Box

15 Caledonian architecture: 2) St. Fillans

and to reduce the clearance volume or dead space in the cylinder ends. In these engines the exhaust ducts round the cylinders were necessarily enlarged and in fact formed a complete steam jacket. The engines had Adams vortex blast pipes, as did many locomotives of the period, and they were in fact quite brilliant performers but they required driving in a much more modern manner than the rest. Drummond did not perpetuate this design because he found it difficult to persuade drivers to use the engines properly and, in any case, the less advanced version was more than equal to the tasks set to it by the services of the period. It is interesting to observe that the steam jacket was not really a good idea, though it may have been a design necessity. The fact is that the temperature of the steam in the jacket, being exhaust steam, would always be lower than the mean temperature of the steam in the cylinder and so heat would be lost through the cylinder wall to the exhaust steam and would disappear uselessly up the chimney. In practice, the loss may have been so small as to be more than outweighed by the more economical working of the valve gear, and the greater freedom in running.

Drummond left in 1890 having done some of the best work of his career, not least in the re-organisation of the workshops. He was succeeded by John Lambie who was already nearing retirement and served for only five years. Lambie was an experienced operator of the Caledonian steam locomotive fleet and, well satisfied with what he had inherited, contented himself with improving on the Drummond boilers. In the races to Edinburgh of 1888, the honours for the northern portion of the West Coast route lay with Drummond's 4-4-0s and with the unique Caledonian single driver, No. 123, which, though designed by its builders, Neilson and Co., followed closely Drummond's designs. In the races to Aberdeen in 1895, it was in fact Lambie's engines, with their slightly freer steaming boilers, which performed the memorable feats. However, the five years of Lambie's superintendency were but a prelude to that of J. F. McIntosh.

There can be no doubt that the high reputation of Caledonian locomotives was earned above all by those of McIntosh, and the entire image of the railway was very largely established by this engineer. It is ironical that the only survivors of his magnificent locomotives are a 0-6-0 freight engine and a 0-4-4 suburban tank, the latter not even built in McIntosh's time. One cannot regret the preservation of the beautiful single driver No. 123, but this was not at all a representative Caledonian locomotive and it is greatly to be regretted that no example of the McIntosh 4-4-0s or 4-6-0s survives to-day. The image of the railway was for long bound up with the famous 4-6-0 'Cardean' which nightly performed on the Anglo-Scottish corridor express, itself an almost unparalleled example of luxury in those splendid sunset years before 1914. The great and graceful blue locomotives coupled to the palatial purple and white carriages with their gold linings, their crests, and their splendid interiors, always seemed to make the Scottish portion of the journey even grander than that south of the Border, because the L.N.W.R. locomotives were considerably less goregous than those of the Caledonian. But, famous though the 4-6-0s were, they were not quite the supreme achievement of McIntosh's career. 'Cardean' and her sisters, including her immediate predecessors, Nos. 49 and 50, were indeed powerful and effective and showed an advance in power over the 4-4-0s. But the 4-4-0s never failed to rise to any challenge presented to them. There were five main groups of these engines. The first engine in the first group was named 'Dunalastair' and looked much like a Lambie or Drummond locomotive except that its boiler was somewhat fatter. In fact McIntosh, who, like Lambie, had been a locomotive running man, had made some changes in the mechanism and had fitted a considerably more powerful boiler. However, the next batch of which the first was named 'Dunalastair 2nd', was again enlarged and provided with a bogie tender. Still small enough to be graceful, this was the type of locomotive which was built for the Belgian State Railways when McIntosh was invited, as a result of his already high standing, to act as consultant. In fact, many locomotives of McIntosh's design appeared on the Belgian railways: 4-4-0s, 0-6-0s, 4-4-2Ts, and even mixed traffic 4-6-0s,

16 McIntosh small wheeled 'Oban Bogie' 4-6-0 leaving Dunblane

all with inside cylinders and closely similar to the contemporary locomotives of the Caledonian. Fortunately, for this reason something very like a 'Dunalastair *2nd*' is preserved in Belgium, though the cab has three side windows in place of the simple curved cutout which was the graceful embellishment of almost all McIntosh tender locomotives.

The third and fourth styles of the 'Dunalastair' family were in turn further enlarged, and with the adoption of superheating, a fifth and most potent of all versions appeared. The great 4-6-0 express engines, starting with Nos. 49 and 50, first appeared after the Dunalastair *2nd* series and represented a very substantial advance in power over those engines. In fact both power and weight were increased by something like 40%. But the superheated 4-4-0s very nearly caught up with the bigger engines, and even when the bigger engines were superheated, there was little to choose between them. So it was that, after the War, big 4-4-0s and 4-6-0s were used turn and turn about on the heaviest trains. The big 4-4-0s were not particularly economical of coal, but their absolute reliability, their mechanical robustness, and their prodigious feats of power output over the severe Caledonian main line, which included the famous climbs to Beattock in both directions, put these engines into the highest class of British locomotive performance before 1914.

McIntosh designed several types of 4-6-0. In addition to the eight express passenger locomotives, there were a number of numerically small classes of mixed traffic engines, some of which could be used in express service, and among them was the small type designed specially for the Oban line. These were in fact the first of his 4-6-0s and were to a most ingenious and effective design, though they needed expert handling. Generally, one cannot avoid the conclusion that the multiplicity of numerically small classes of 4-6-0s indicated that McIntosh was not wholly satisfied with any of them but in this he was like other designers of the period, such as J. G. Robinson of the Great Central. The

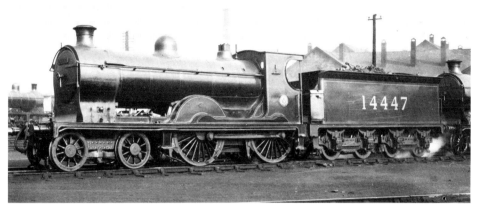

17 A superheated 'Dunalastair IV' in L.M.S. colours

fact is that it was not easy to progress from a 4-4-0 to a 4-6-0, and also that during the period of all this activity higher axle loads became acceptable so that the recourse to 3-coupled axles ceased to be necessary for many types of service. This explains the not uncommon experience on British railways that heavy superheated 4-4-0s were fully capable of handling the trains for which non-superheated 4-6-0s had at one time been provided.

McIntosh may also have been responsible for the first full-length, freight trains fitted throughout with continuous brakes. Under his regime, a number of such sets were provided and 0-8-0 locomotives were built to handle them. He also built 8-coupled shunting tanks, while his standard 0-6-0 was steadily improved and included one batch designated for passenger service and painted accordingly in the rich blue livery. Eventually, a small group was built with leading carrying wheels, an inside cylinder 2-6-0 which rode steadily at speed and was to inspire an enlarged version on the Glasgow & South Western.

McIntosh retired in 1914 and the rest of the Caledonian locomotive story was less distinguished though it did contain one bizarre incident. This was the acquisition of six large 4-6-0s from the Highland Railway. These, intended to be the Highland 'River' class, were locomotives of far more modern appearance than any others in Scotland, with two outside cylinders, Walschaert's valve gear, Belpaire fireboxes and various other features which were to become familiar in the more recent history of British railways. They had been designed by F. G. Smith but had been found to be too heavy when delivered from their makers. This kind of thing had happened before and was usually due to a civil engineer having second thoughts when he saw in solid metal something which had not alarmed him on paper. In the case of these engines, however, the Highland board took fright and sold them (at a profit) to the Caledonian while Smith was asked to resign. And so the Caledonian received what some of its employees regarded as the finest 4–6–0s ever to run in Scotland.

Such distinction, however, did not attach to the locomotives of McIntosh's successor, William Pickersgill. Pickersgill was a quiet and polite man, less of a 'character' than his predecessor, and he came from a small and quiet railway, the Great North of Scotland. He was perhaps a little too old though he remained in the seat for the nine years that remained

18 A Pickersgill 4-4-0 at Perth in 1922

of the Caledonian's independent existence. He continued building 4-4-0s and 0-6-0s, both types being made even more massively than the previous examples, but these engines never had the sparkle of the earlier ones. However, they were built to last and last they did, right to the end of steam, though no outstanding feats were recorded of them. Pickersgill's 4-6-0s were of three types and the first of these, the No. 60 class, was a general purpose machine having outside cylinders but inside steam chests and valve gear. Further examples of this design were built by L.M.S. immediately after the Grouping. They were at their best on fitted freight trains. As passenger engines they were remarkably sluggish and were apt to lose time for no apparent reason. But they were also extremely strongly built and had long if undistinguished lives. Their nickname was 'The Greybacks'. Whether this was due to their soiling their boilers in early days as a result of a tendency to prime, or whether it was simply an insult, nobody will now know for certain. But it is worth pointing out that 'Greyback' is a common Scottish word for wood louse. The other Pickersgill 4-6-0s were a small engine for the Oban line, with outside cylinders and Walschaert's gear—a kind of reduced version of the ex-Highland locomotives but not at all favourably viewed by the men that had to operate it; and the last, and most magnificent looking of all Caledonian express locomotives, the three cylinder 956 class, of which only three were built. Great care had been lavished on their appearance, and seldom has the look of power been more harmoniously clothed, but, sad to relate, they were utter failures.

So, on a note of decline ended the once magnificent Caledonian locomotive development. But most of the McIntosh locomotives continued for many years to show their class, albeit in the red livery of the L.M.S., and Pickersgill's 4-4-0s were to be seen in the last years of steam traction wearing the elaborately lined black livery which British Railways had revived from the L.N.W.R.

It is of course the trains that attract most attention, and of which the memory is most vividly kept alive by the photographs and the old posters, so many of which have been preserved. The Caledonian was a railway more than it was a shipping line, but extended reference is made to the maritime rivalry between it and the Glasgow & South Western in the chapter relating to that railway and we may here draw attention to the fact that the

19 Pickersgill's best design, the Wemyss Bay tank

Caledonian, like some other railway companies, had in its employ or on its Board of Directors, a number of people of extremely strong character and personality. Among those mention must be made of Captain James Williamson, the marine superintendent. He had made his name as the enterprising and courageous captain of a Clyde steamer, the 'Sultana'. He had a great following among the public who made use of the steamer services and was in fact quite a celebrity. The Caledonian Railway recognised the high spirits and energy of this man and appointed him marine superintendent in 1889. And as with that other larger-than-life character, J. F. McIntosh, the company fully supported him by providing him with the finest possible equipment for his task and allowing him the greatest freedom in matters of design.

The tracks of the Caledonian were almost all double and well laid. There was here little of that image of so many Scottish railways, the image of single tracks winding endlessly through remote and scarcely populated regions. Perhaps the Caledonian brought traffic and population to the areas it served, or perhaps its shrewd directors never sought to create new traffics but only to tap the potential implicit in the geography of the country. The most sensational piece of civil engineering was probably the Connel Ferry Viaduct, which was not on an important main line but was in a rather romantic setting in the West Highlands. Among the stations it was undoubtedly the Glasgow Central Station which, after re-organisation at the beginning of the 20th century, represented the greatest feat of building construction. Because the trains were above street level, in order to provide for shipping to pass beneath over the Clyde which lay immediately outside the Station, there was an immensely strong floor capable of taking the weight of many locomotives at once and, in its time, this building work, which included provision for nine tracks crossing the Clyde, was regarded as a major feat of engineering. Undoubtedly the Caledonian in this period of its existence was doing things on a lavish scale and the heritage which it left at the Grouping has been of enormous value to its successors. In Edinburgh also, the Princes Street Station was enlarged and modernised, as was the joint station at Aberdeen.

Unfortunately, there is one incident which cannot be left out of the story of the Caledonian. The worst railway disaster ever to take place in the British Isles took place on its metals in 1915. No other pre-Grouping railway is so strongly associated with a particular accident as the Caledonian is with that at Quintinshill, near Gretna Green. In that accident, there was nothing wrong with the track or the signalling or the locomotives and rolling stock involved. The disaster was entirely due to the incredible negligence of several of the company's servants. Three trains were involved, one of them a troop train which ran at high speed into a stationary local train headed by the most immovable obstacle which the Caledonian ever put on rails, a 'Cardean' class 4-6-0. The troop train was made of wooden carriages, gas lit, and was running under clear signals at some 70 miles per hour. In the collision its length was reduced to one-third. Less than one minute later the pile of wreckage was run into by a heavy, double-headed night express from London to Glasgow. The pile of wreckage was unbelievable, and, because the gas tanks were lit from the burning coals of the overturned locomotive, the whole lot burned for 24 hours. Two hundred and twenty-seven people died and this record has never yet been approached by any other railway accident in Britain, though the roads take this toll every fortnight.

The disaster really had nothing to do with the War, and in other respects the Caledonian showed up remarkably well during this period. It had to take vast loads of coal and other supplies over its system before handing them over to the Highland Railway for further transportation, ultimately to the Fleet at Scapa Flow. Although train services were slow inevitably, the magnificent liveries of locomotives and carriages were preserved throughout the entire period. Two of the splendid steamers of the Caledonian Steam Packet Company were sunk on War service but all the rest of the fleet returned to the Clyde after the War. The general standard of maintenance, cleanliness of stations and punctuality was well maintained and the railway entered its brief period of post-War existence with its image undimmed by the hard tasks it had performed. And when the Grouping took place, the organisation of the L.M.S. group, of which it formed a part, reflected its pre-eminence in the northern part of the new system. Caledonian officers filled almost all the senior posts and so took charge of the Glasgow & South Western and the Highland Railways. In fact, the Grouping achieved for the Caledonian that hegemony over half of Scotland which it had never quite managed to achieve for itself.

The story of the Caledonian began in 1836 when, a year before its opening, the Grand Junction Railway, one of the constituent members of the L.N.W.R., had despatched Joseph Locke, the engineer, to assess the possibilities of a railway from Lancashire through Carlisle to Glasgow and Edinburgh. The disputes over rival routes between Lancaster and Carlisle were solved without too much bitterness but it was not so easy with the rival routes in Scotland. There were two possible routes for the new line, one via Annandale and over Beattock summit to Edinburgh and Glasgow (which later became the Caledonian line), the other via Nithsdale and Dumfries to Glasgow only, (later a part of the Glasgow & South Western). Locke, overawed by the formidable Beattock summit and supported by Glasgow merchants, favoured the Nithsdale route, but two Scottish worthies, J. J. Hope-Johnstone and Charles Stewart were pressing for the more direct route via Annandale and were busy enlisting the support of the Grand Junction and the Lancaster & Preston Railways in England. In 1844, the name, the Caledonian Railway, carefully concealing the English associations of the Hope-Johnstone, Stewart bloc, was first adopted for the Annandale route and in 1845 the Annandale party won the battle for the authorisation of its line. The bill sanctioning the Caledonian Railway passed through Parliament in July and authorised a line from Carlisle to Garriongill Junction to link with the mineral lines already in existence around Glasgow; another line from Cumbernauld to Castlecary; and a third line from Carstairs to Edinburgh. The whole network, including the ascent of Beattock summit, 1014 ft., was completed by 1848 and connections made with a series of smaller companies, some already in existence, others planned by Locke and Brassey, to take the line through to Greenock, Perth and Aberdeen. The Companies concerned, including among the existing lines the Dundee & Newtyle, the Dundee & Arbroath and the Arbroath & Forfar; and among the Brassey, Locke lines, the Scottish Midland (Perth to Forfar), the Scottish Central (Castlecary to Perth), and the Aberdeen Railway (Friockheim to Aberdeen), all eventually became a part of the Caledonian. First to be absorbed was the Scottish Central, in 1865 embracing Perth, Dundee, Alloa and Callander, and this was followed in 1866 by the Scottish North Eastern linking Aberdeen, Montrose, Stanley and Perth.

The concept of the company was therefore a grand one, but it was nevertheless an English one and however much the Caledonian might develop its own character and charm the English influence was to remain a distinctive feature of the company's affairs.

Like many other young railway companies both in England and in Scotland the Caledonian was soon to find itself in serious financial difficulties, the problems arising principally through the failure of the company to build its line right into Glasgow, and through its early involvement in the extension of lines to Perth and Aberdeen. Both meant a serious drain on revenues, the one in tolls to the chain of local railways linking Garriongill Junction to the station in Glasgow, the other in capital for the engineering works on the northern lines. The situation was only aggravated by the Caledonian's insistence on senseless competition with the much more direct Edinburgh & Glasgow Railway, itself already in difficulties through running its 3rd class service at the ridiculously low fare of 6d.!

By November 1849, dissatisfaction with the affairs of the company was mounting. There were proposals for amalgamating with the L.N.W.R. but these came to nought and finally the English shareholders (in the majority on the Caledonian board) took matters into their own hands, seizing railway property by way of compensation and forcing the resignation of Hope-Johnstone. Captain Plunket, the leader of the English committee, took his place as General Manager and ordered a full investigation of the companies affairs. Following a letter of reassurance to all debenture holders and a substantial infusion of capital and confidence from the millionaire iron-master, James Baird, the Caledonian was well on the way to recovery and to becoming a highly respected Scottish railway with efficient services, good stations and comfortable steamers; a fitting partner for the Premier Line.

The early expansion of the Caledonian had taken the form of an amalgamation with the Glasgow, Paisley & Greenock Railway in 1851, to open up exciting possibilities for Caledonian steamer services to Dunoon, the Gareloch, Holy Loch, and Rothesay. At first the Caledonian was the only major railway company in the area, although competition was rife from private steam packet companies. In 1865, however, the year the Caledonian saw the opening of the Wemyss Bay Railway to give it a second port on the Clyde, its old rival the Glasgow & South Western gained a foothold in the area with the authorisation of the

Greenock & Ayrshire Railway, linking Greenock with the G.S.W.R. line at Johnstone. Opened in 1869, it was soon winning traffic from the Caledonian because of its more convenient terminal station at Greenock. Another competitor, the North British, began steam boat operations in 1866, but the Caledonian sensibly refrained from embarking on expensive rival developments until 1882-9 when the Greenock to Gourock line was built, giving the Caledonian a 3 mile advantage over its rivals. There was still some very exciting competition, though, with the steamers of the three companies, the 'Caley', the G.S.W.R. and the N.B.R. vying with each other to be first at Dunoon.

Further north, the Caley had links with an independent steamer service from Oban to the Hebrides, via the Callander & Oban line authorised in 1865, but not built till much later. The financial affairs of this company, however, were none too good and consequently the Highland Railway's protege, the Dingwall & Skye, opened its steamer port at Strome Ferry ten years before the Callander & Oban line was opened in 1880. Nevertheless, Oban was a rich prize for the Caledonian in terms of tourist traffic both to the picturesque town itself and to the Hebridean islands.

To the south, in the depths of G.S.W.R. territory, the Caledonian operated another steamer service from Ardrossan to the Isle of Arran via the Lanarkshire & Ayrshire Railway. This was an independent concern authorised in 1883-4, but worked and maintained by the Caledonian. This meant that by 1888 the Caledonian had gained access to Ardrossan town and by 1890 to Ardrossan pier to begin competition with the G.S.W.R., an event marked by the introduction of the fine new steamer, the Duchess of Hamilton.

On the east coast, the emphasis of the company's business was slightly different because of its large export trade to Russia and Europe. Dealing mainly in the coal and iron products of Lanarkshire and Stirlingshire, the company had in 1867 bought two small docks and associated canals at Grangemouth, with the intention of developing a servicable port. It was in fact to use the Forth and Clyde canal for pleasure sailing but obviously its main interest in the area was commercial. The acquisition was an important one, for between 1867 and 1876 trade through the port more than doubled. Additional dock space was necessary in 1876 and again in 1897 and by 1906 the Caledonian was handling over 3 million tons of merchandise and minerals at Grangemouth.

The tourist traffic potential of the railway, with its links to romantic Scottish highlands and islands, was immense and no effort was spared to attract passengers. The Caledonian was also renowned for its part in the London to Edinburgh and London to Aberdeen races of 1888 and 1895 and for its place in the day-to-day running of the Anglo-Scottish trains. It was in fact, a great compliment to the company that the Queen should so frequently travel to Balmoral via the West Coast and the Caledonian, taking her breakfast in the station hotel at Perth. Punctuality was an advertised characteristic, and with non-stop runs of over a hundred miles between Carlisle and Edinburgh and Carlisle and Glasgow, the Caledonian completed its part of the journey in an average of 130 minutes.

After the West Coast service, the Grampian Express, introduced in 1905 to run between Glasgow and Aberdeen, is probably the best known and best loved of the Caledonian passenger trains. New, luxurious coaches, built specifically for this service, proved something of a sensation in Scotland, being spacious 12-wheeled carriages, 68 ft. long, with high curved roofs on the G.W.R. pattern. The 3rd class accommodation was excellent with peacock blue upholstered seats for four persons each side in corridor coaches, while

20 Perhaps the oldest station in Scotland, Dundee, Dundee & Newtyle Railway

the 1st class compartments seated three aside. It was in fact the Grampian Express, together with the gradient profile of the Carlisle–Glasgow route, which appeared on the famous Caledonian publicity bookmark issued by the company to promote its best services.

In 1893 the Caley absorbed the Wemyss Bay Railway and straightway began improvements to the line and terminal station. The completed station was outstanding even by the high standards of the Caledonian. Not only were the platforms long and spacious but the glass covered circulating area was pleasantly decorated with hanging baskets full of geraniums. Stations at Stirling, Oban and Strathyre also bore the unmistakable elegance of the Caledonian.

The Engineers-in-chief of the company, George Graham from 1853-1899, and Donald Matheson from 1899-1910, were responsible for supervising the development of the track and maintaining the high standards of Joseph Locke. In the 1880s Graham presided over the Greenock–Gourock extension line and the building of the underground Glasgow Central Railway, authorised in 1888. The engineering work involved in the building of this line, planned to link the heavy industrial areas of S.E. Glasgow with the canal and dock properties of the west, was immense. The work commenced in 1890 and took six years to complete.

In 1895 the Caledonian took over the Solway Junction Railway running from Kirtlebridge to Brayton, bypassing Carlisle and proving very valuable for bringing iron-ore to the iron-works in Lanarkshire. Two years later the company was busy improving its steamer berthing facilities at Oban and beginning construction of a single branch line to Ballaculish in an attempt to attract yet more traffic.

The vigour and stature of the Caledonian at the close of the 19th and the beginning of the 20th century, was nowhere better evidenced than in its two imposing new stations at Edinburgh and Glasgow. New Princes Street station in Edinburgh, replacing a temporary structure of 1870, was built between 1890 and 1893. It was, at last, a suitably grand station for the Scottish capital, with seven operating platforms, a fine bayed roof 850 ft. long and a fine entry arch. The rebuilt Glasgow Central station was perhaps even more impressive. Permission to enlarge the station was granted in 1899 and the Caledonian put into operation its plans for doubling the passenger accommodation and increasing the length of the platforms. It says something for the determination and organisational skill of the company, that the work, including a new nine track bridge across the Clyde, should be completed in six years and that during the alterations, traffic into Glasgow Central should actually increase.

The Caledonian railway approached the war and subsequently the Grouping as an efficient and much admired railway, entrusted with the Royal Mails, a suitable associate for the 'Premier Line' to the south, and an essential link in the economic structure of Great Britain.

There is no <u>BETTER WAY</u>

TO

The Picturesque and Romantic

<u>HIGHLANDS OF SCOTAND,</u>

THE EVER CHARMING

<u>CLYDE COAST RESORTS</u>

OF THE LOWLANDS,

And the other <u>DELIGHTFUL DISTRICTS</u>

OF

<u>BONNIE SCOTLAND</u>

THAN BY

<u>The Caledonian Railway,</u>

THE TRUE LINE OF WAY.

Pass of Brander, Loch Awe.

Major Routes of the
Glasgow and South Western Railway

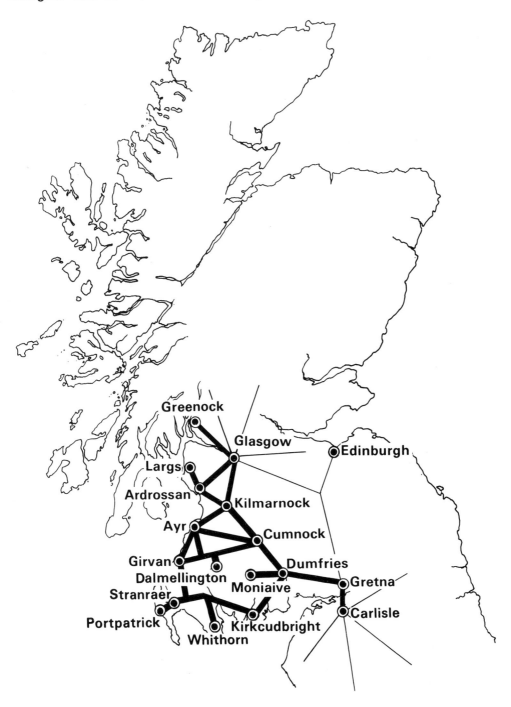

Greenock

Glasgow

Edinburgh

Largs

Ardrossan

Kilmarnock

Ayr

Cumnock

Girvan

Dumfries

Dalmellington

Moniaive

Gretna

Stranraer

Carlisle

Portpatrick

Kirkcudbright

Whithorn

thin lines indicate other connecting railways

44

The Glasgow & South Western Railway

21 The Glasgow & South Western and the Midland at Carlisle Citadel Station

The traveller to Glasgow from London had three main choices of route, which entailed leaving the English capital from Euston, St. Pancras or Kings Cross. Those in a hurry usually chose Euston but those who were more self-indulgent usually chose St. Pancras. One had to have some very special reason to go to Glasgow from Kings Cross. The attraction of St. Pancras was probably the luxury of the Anglo Scottish rolling stock which was operated from that station. It was, of course, of Midland design but many of the vehicles were lettered 'M & GSW'. This was the central route alternative to the East Coast or West Coast Joint Stock. Another possible attraction of the central route was undoubtedly the dramatic landscape through which it passed north of Leeds as it climbed to the Pennine summit at Ais Gill and then dropped down to Carlisle but, a little to the north of Carlisle at Gretna Junction, the train would be on the metals of one of the smaller and poorer railways in the British Isles. However, the Glasgow & South Western was a railway full of character and pride and could be counted upon to make up for the consequences of its poverty by the energy and esprit de corps with which it ran its business. The locomotive which it provided to take over the 'Diner' from England might well be as impressive as those of its great rival, the Caledonian, over whose tracks the G.S.W. was obliged to take its trains for the first few miles north and on the footplate there was certainly a determination to prove that the smaller railway could do anything as well as the big railway if it tried.

It has no doubt been pointed out before that the grouping of the railways in 1923 only began to be a reality in the minds of the railway employees twenty-five years later when the groups to which they had never been able to give much loyalty ceased to exist at the moment of nationalisation. So much is natural human perversity. But the L.M.S. aroused less company loyalty even than the L.N.E.R. or the Southern, and the traditional suspicion which, in Scotland, was undoubtedly greatest between the Glasgow & South Western and Caledonian, survived nationalisation by a good many years. Anything that went wrong in the nationalised system in the south of Scotland was traditionally blamed on to the continuing presence of ex-Caledonian men on the railway. Perhaps one might say that the old 'Sou' West' had a chip on its shoulder. But this chip undoubtedly was made heavier by the policies of the newly formed L.M.S. The style of management, unlike that of the L.N.E.R., the Southern, or the Great Western, showed absolutely no sensitivity to local feelings and loyalties and no realisation of the extent to which the prosperity of the railway depended upon the triangular relationship between the public, the companies' servants, and the management. The L.M.S., for what appeared to be sound economic reasons, introduced a policy of locomotive standardisation which entailed the premature scrapping of many pre-grouping types and in this the Glasgow & South Western locomotive stock suffered more than any other. The replacement machines were often Caledonian, because those were more numerous and, in any case, Caledonian men had very largely been put in charge of the G. & S.W.R. The rancour between the servants of the two companies was probably greater after the grouping than ever it was before.

There was really no comparison between the two railways but there was a certain amount of territorial rivalry. The title of the smaller company accurately described the territory it served, whereas that of the larger one was vague and imposing and unspecific. The smaller company connected Glasgow to Carlisle and also to the Ayrshire coast and to places on the Clyde Estuary. It operated the Portpatrick & Wigtownshire Railway, known as the 'Port' Road, jointly with the Caledonian and so ran Irish boat trains to Stranraer. The Irish boat train was normally referred to as the 'Paddy'. The Caledonian did not pay much attention to this southwestern tip of Scotland, but did have a short branch from its Carlisle–Glasgow main line to Dumfries. Further north, however, it thrust a long and intricate finger into South Western territory with its line to Ardrossan, a place also served by the South Western. From there, both companes ran steamer services to the Isle of Aran and it was a wonder they did not sink each other. Along the Clyde Estuary, though there was traffic enough for three railways and three railways to share it, there was still a fair tangle between the rivals around Greenock.

Both railways operated Clyde Steamers in later years. The rivalry was intense and the vessels of both companies were beautiful. There was much actual neck and neck racing,

22 Glasgow St. Enoch Station, G. & S.W.R

and the victory was often a matter of sheer nerve and skilled handling of the craft by their helmsmen, to ensure priority at a landing stage. The passengers, naturally enough, were strongly partisan, and regulars were firm in their allegiances. In general, the view was that though the Caledonian vessels were luxurious, those of the 'Sou'-West' were swifter and more graceful, but each addition to either fleet altered the balance.

Although the South Western had an impressive Glasgow terminus, St. Enoch, the real heart of the system was Kilmarnock and it was there that the railway company had its locomotive works. From there all the important lines seemed to radiate and though it was possible to by-pass this centre by a route further to the west, most trains that could possibly serve Kilmarnock did so. Another important railway centre and junction was at Ayr but this was little exploited as a port for passenger services. Dumfries was the junction at which one arrived from Carlisle and from which, if one wished to cross the Irish Sea to Larne, one's train left the route to Glasgow and took the line towards Kirkcudbright, at a point along which one's train was diverted on to the Port Road for a long and somewhat tortuous journey across the irregular southern-most coastline of Scotland. None of these places was a source of particularly lucrative traffic but there was sufficient commercial activity in the triangle formed by Ayr, Kilmarnock and Ardrossan to provide a useful supplement to that derived from Glasgow itself.

This part of the British Isles is rumoured to have an exceptionally mild climate but, whereas this may be true just a little further north, the Gulf Stream does not seem to have so benign an influence down here, and the 'Port Road' as well as the railway which follows the coastline down from Ayr to join it, were both snowed up occasionally in hard winters, as well as the routes inland. The railway also had some very severely graded routes. On the main line between Carlisle and Glasgow there was a long and gruelling

23 Manson 4-6-0, No. 386, then new, at Carlisle

climb halfway between Dumfries and Kilmarnock to the summit of New Cumnock, and the end of the route, north of Kilmarnock, entering Glasgow, was sharply undulating and difficult. In fact, there was hardly any part of the railway that was actually easy to work except possibly the section from Gretna to Dumfries. Elsewhere it was all steep climbs and many of the routes had many sharp curves as well. The route from Glasgow to Greenock was not only difficult but also had to be worked at the highest possible speed, because it served G.S.W. steamer services subject to very keen competition. This was the one route which gave its name in popular parlance to the locomotives designed to work it, and there were 'Greenock bogies', just as the Caledonian had 'Oban bogies'.

The locomotive stock developed over the years was very characteristic of the railway and its physical limitations. There was always a large number of tiny 0-4-0 locomotives with four-wheeled tenders. The earliest of these were of Bury design and were built in 1841 for the Glasgow, Paisley, Kilmarnock & Ayr Railway, which was the forerunner of the G.S.W., the latter title first appearing in 1850. The last 0-4-0 tender locomotives were built to the design of James Stirling in the early 1870s. There were twenty-two of these and they had an average life of fifty years. That so many and such small locomotives were found to be useful right up to the end of the railway's independent existence gives a clear indication of the nature of some of the industrial and agricultural branch lines with which locomotives had to contend. Rather curiously, although the railway was not, until its last years, at all fond of tank locomotives, the heaviest of all British 0-4-0 tanks, at least on the main line railways, were six built by James Manson in 1907-1909. These engines weighed no less than 39 tons 12 cwt. on a wheel base of only 7 ft. 6 ins., and were built mainly for service at Greenock Harbour where extremely sharp curves were combined with 1 in 50 gradients.

24 An old Stirling 0-4-2, well preserved and well cherished

The 0-4-2 tender engine was also a favourite during most of the railway's existence and well into the L.M.S. period. The first of these were again of Bury design and appeared in 1848, but the type was perpetuated by Patrick Stirling in several successive batches and by his brother James. Indeed, of James' last essay in the type, sixty engines built between 1874 and 1878, some survived in their original form to 1929. Half of them were re-built by Manson and did excellent work including quite important passenger trains, right up to the end of the railway's independent existence. But, of course, this type was originally conceived as a goods locomotive and remained the most satisfactory engine for this kind of service on the more tortuous routes. The re-builds were most attractive machines, not dissimilar to the Adams 'Jubilees' which had such long and useful lives on the London & South Western. Although this wheel arrangement was found on other railways, it was certainly a characteristic of the two 'South Western' systems in more recent years.

The Glasgow & South Western was a line with heavy mineral traffic, some of which originated in mines in its own area but quite a lot of which was in transit from South Wales to the Clyde and coast ports. The 0-6-0 wheel arrangement appeared with engines built at Kilmarnock to the design of Patrick Stirling in 1862 and 1863. Originally these engines had weather boards only but the characteristic Stirling cab was added later and the domeless boiler was there from the start. A few years later another six of an enlarged type were built at Kilmarnock and twenty similar by Neilsons. The first of these appeared in the very year in which their designer moved to the Great Northern and attention has been paid to these two rather obscure classes of locomotive because they were Stirling's first essays in the type. Some of his other locomotives for the G.S.W., such as the 0-4-2s and the outside cylinder 2-2-2s, pre-figured his later and more famous designs. There is no doubt that Stirling was not only the designer of very beautiful looking locomotives but also of some of the finest and most trouble-free, and it is interesting to observe that he learned valuable lessons on the hard roads of South West Scotland. It is also interesting to note that he nearly trebled his salary, to £2,000 a year, when he went to the Great Northern.

Stirling's brother James, fifteen years his junior, succeeded him on the G.S.W. and produced one class of twelve 0-6-0s. They were good engines and the last of them was fifty years old when the L.M.S. withdrew it in 1928. But the most numerous class of 0-6-0 was due to Hugh Smellie. Mostly built by the railway, they appeared between 1881 and 1890, and some of them were re-built by R. H. Whitelegg in the last years of the company's existence and these re-builds survived well into the 1930s. Smellie's successor, James Manson, built a further twenty of them with only the slightest of alterations and these were succeeded by several series of 0-6-0s to Manson's own design, eventually totalling sixty-seven. One of these engines passed into the service of the National Coal Board in comparatively recent years, having originally been sold as far back as 1926 to a colliery in Northumberland. She was still in existence in Coal Board service as late as 1949 but was unfortunately broken up just before an effort was made to preserve her as the last surviving tender locomotive of the Glasgow & South Western. So it was that the only engine to be found to represent the old company was a rather unrepresentative 0-6-0 shunting tank of Whitelegg's design, and one must regret that the most typical of the locomotives of the railway, a Manson 4-4-0, does not to-day stand in the Transport Museum in Glasgow.

The 0-6-0s ended with a batch of fifteen engines designed by Peter Drummond. Built by the North British Locomotive Company in 1913, none lasted for more than twenty years. They were extremely heavy and sluggish machines which, though they had the power to slog up gradients with fifty wagons behind them, were not normally allowed to do so because they were so painfully slow. They also had a most extraordinary tendency to overheating. Their fuel consumption sometimes reached 120 lbs. per mile. Known as the 'pumpers' because they were fitted with feed pumps and feed water heaters in the tenders, they should have been provided with superheat, but this was possibly excluded on grounds of weight as they were already the heaviest of their kind in the British Isles, weighing nearly 58 tons. Yet, for all their faults, they were in a sense the detested progenitor of a greatly loved offspring, because virtually the same design, but provided with superheat and a leading truck appeared from 1915. The Drummond inside cylinder 2-6-0s incorporated all the lessons in detail design that could be derived from their unhappy predecessors. They were in fact magnificent locomotives, only 4 tons heavier but much more economical in coal, much more free-running, and said to be a delight to drive and to fire. They were the last of the survivors in normal service of the Glasgow & South Western tender locomotive stock, the last being withdrawn in March 1947.

No apology is made for dealing with the passenger engines after those used in freight service, because the latter earned most of the money. But the passenger engines were more in the public eye and their exploits were more dashing. The Glasgow, Paisley, Kilmarnock & Ayr Railway had some 2-2-0 Bury locomotives and some 2-2-2s, mostly of the Stephenson patentee type. Shortly before 1850 some more sophisticated locomotives were built including a number of the standard Hawthorn design, identical to some supplied to the Great Northern. But the greatest interest in the early years inevitably centres on the engines of Patrick Stirling. Stirling's 2-2-2s for the G.S.W. were not in fact the forerunners of his 2-2-2 for the G.N.R. but much more of his celebrated 8 ft. singles. They had outside cylinders placed horizontally, and were not unlike the products of Crewe except that they had single inside frames. To start with they had no cabs at all, merely weather boards, and later they received simple side sheets bent over to form a roof with a porthole window in each side. They did not last very long, but that was normal for the express

25 James Stirling's celebrated 4-4-0

engines of the fifties and sixties, because train weights were increasing very rapidly and the engines were soon inadequate for the tasks set to them. They were also unsuited to the secondary duties or slow freight to which they might otherwise have been relegated and so their lives were inevitably rather shortened.

James Stirling did not share his brother's tenacious loyalty to the single driver for the principal passenger services, and built a range of excellent 2-4-0s before bringing out the locomotives for which his period on the Glasgow & South Western is best known. These were, of course, the twenty-two 4-4-0s built at Kilmarnock between 1873 and 1877. Although these engines only lasted some twenty years in their original state, those that were re-built by Stirling's successors lasted into the late 1920s, so there must have been excellent material and some excellent features of design in them. These locomotives were justly famous, being very large for their period, with 18 inch cylinders and 7 ft. 1 in. drivers and a grate area of 16 sq. ft. They were among the first 4-4-0s in the British Isles, though the Wheatley bogies on the North British ante-dated them. They were not quite the standard British 4-4-0 because their short wheel base bogie had a fixed pivot—a rather inexplicable feature when one remembers that William Adams had introduced his design of bogie with lateral play controlled by springs several years earlier. All the same, this 39 ton locomotive was a very large advance on the immediately preceeding passenger locomotives, 2-4-0 or 2-2-2, which had turned the scale at around 30 tons (without tenders in all cases). The Manson re-builds gave excellent service for many years. These Stirling 4-4-0s had very deep valances from end to end incorporating coupling rod splashers, they had domeless boilers and the Stirling family's characteristic cab as seen on the Great Northern. Their appearance was very closely followed in the 4-4-0s which Stirling built for the South Eastern Railway, to which he moved in 1878.

For the next twelve years Hugh Smellie reigned at Kilmarnock. Smellie had come from the little Maryport & Carlisle and his translation to the much bigger G.S.W. was a major promotion indeed. He entirely justified the confidence placed in him and all his locomotives were first class, while his passenger locomotives could reasonably be described as magnificent. He started off rather surprisingly with a large 2-4-0 design of which twelve were built in 1879 and 1880. These engines were of virtually the same weight and certainly the same power as Stirling's bogies, though their driving wheels were 3 or 4 ins. smaller. The use of a single leading axle with rather large wheels in place of the bogie may well have been required by the lengths of turntables at certain points on the routes to which

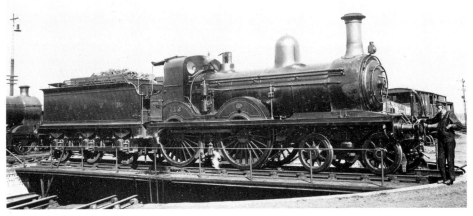

26 Originally designed by Hugh Smellie for working boat trains, this excellent old engine was still in pre-Grouping colours when photographed at Carstairs in 1926

the locomotives were drafted—for instance, the turntable at Stranraer could not accommodate the 4-4-0 and some of these large 2-4-0s were immediately used on the Glasgow–Stranraer trains. It was perhaps inevitable that, as bigger turntables were installed, engines with leading bogies would eventually supplant them on the faster services, in view of the tortuous nature of so many of the G.S.W. main lines. Seven years later Smellie brought out his larger-wheeled 4-4-0s, which were some 3 tons heavier and had slightly enlarged dimensions. There are those who claim that this was the finest express engine ever produced for the railway and even those in original conditions had lives of 35 to 40 years while those which received the attentions of Manson or Whitelegg lasted considerably longer. However, the immediately preceeding Smellie 4-4-0 design, which was closely similar, was perhaps held in even greater affection. These engines were the 'Wee Bogies' of which there were twenty-two, and though their grates were slightly smaller and their driving wheels only 6 ft. 1 in. in diameter, their cylinders were as large and their actual performances in no way inferior to those of the nominally larger engines except, inevitably, in the matter of absolute maximum speed.

Hugh Smellie left the Glasgow & South Western in the summer of 1890. He had been appointed to succeed Dugald Drummond on the Caledonian Railway. This was a recognition by the most prosperous of the Scottish railways of Smellie's outstanding qualities and it is sad to recall that he was unable to develop his ideas because he died less than a year later, the consequence of spending a long winter's night superintending a breakdown gang. He was only 50 years old but he had not been very fit for some years. His place was taken by James Manson, who came from the Great North of Scotland Railway, but, like Smellie, had had a previous career and considerable advancement, on the railway to which he was now appointed.

Manson stayed for 21 years and his locomotives were perhaps those most characteristic of the line. He departed from the previous mechanical standards in many respects, but not in such a way as to arouse the hostility of the operating staff. A characteristic of Manson's engines was that he placed balanced slide valves on top of the inside cylinders, and they were driven via rocking levers. The Drummond tradition so influential on Scottish

27 Manson's four cylinder engine of 1897, when new

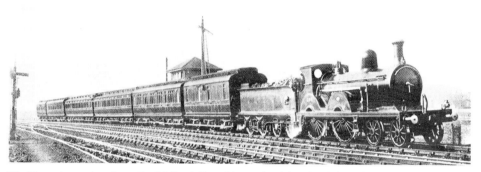

28 Through coaches from the Midland. Note Manson's eight wheeled tender

railways retained the arrangement of slide valves between cylinders, though Drummond himself did much to overcome the disadvantages of this situation in ways which are detailed in the chapter on the Caledonian. But, as cylinders became larger it was obvious that the place for the valves would have to move and though Drummond himself was very tardy in acknowledging this fact, Manson led the way in his large wheeled 4-4-0 class introduced in 1892. There were 57 of them eventually and, as built, they were lively and economical machines though generally limited to loads of about 160 tons on the fastest schedules. But then, they only weighed 45 tons without their tenders. They were also very elegant little machines, much more so than those of Smellie, but closely resembling Manson's engines on the G.N. of S. Also from his previous appointment Manson introduced an eight-wheeled tender having an inside frame bogie at the front end and four wheels carried in the main tender frames at the rear. Two of these large tenders were used on the locomotives reserved for working the 'Pullman' between Glasgow and Carlisle, because this train did not necessarily stop at Dumfries and a large water capacity was needed.

Twenty-five of a smaller-wheeled version were built between 1895 and 1899. They had an increased boiler pressure, and this, in conjunction with the smaller driving wheel, gave

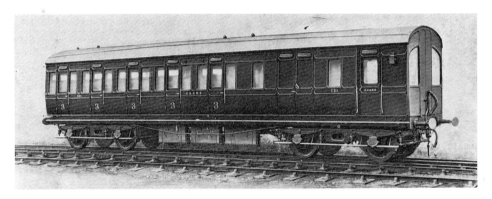

29 Brake third coach, circa 1910

them an increased tractive effort. They were built originally for the Greenock Road, which had also been the reason for Smellie's 'Wee Bogies'. These engines were, if anything, even more lively and economical than the big-wheeled ones. In the fullness of time, increasing train loads obliged Manson to bring out a larger boilered version of his express 4-4-0, with a higher pressure but retaining the chassis unchanged. There were fifteen of these and still later a further batch with an entirely different type of boiler followed them, in which the deep, short firebox was replaced by a longer shallow box in which the grate sloped up over the rear axle.

It is sad to report that these really excellent Manson 4-4-0s all suffered at the hands of his successors. In the case of Peter Drummond, who came first, they suffered mainly neglect, and when R. H. Whitelegg took over he found that the toll of the heavy War-time traffic, on top of the previous neglect, had left him with engines very largely in the process of repair. Unfortunately, Whitelegg did not allow them to be repaired to their original admirable design, but instituted a series of standard alterations which included new boiler designs fitted to some, and, even worse, an alteration in the design of the valve gear which was applied to very many Manson engines including all the Greenock bogies. This piece of re-design was possibly conceived in a laudable effort to reduce maintenance, but it was wholly disastrous. As re-built the engines were sluggish and shy for steam and only the brilliant Greenock bogies still had enough virtue left in them to perform usefully. This was the state of affairs discovered by the L.M.S. when it took over and perhaps goes some way towards explaining the fact that the engines of the G. & S.W. disappeared faster even than those of any other constituent of the new railway. It is only fair to Whitelegg to point out that the one locomotive which he designed from scratch, the Baltic tank, was a very good engine indeed.

Almost as characteristic an image of the G. & S.W. was provided by Manson's 4-6-0s. These suffered in exactly the same way, and at the same hands and their reputation was a very bad one at the time of the grouping. But when they were new and properly looked after they were very satisfactory, and the two examples of the superheated version were positively excellent. Manson designed his 4-6-0 in 1901 though the first did not appear until early in 1903. The order went to Sharp, Stewart & Company but the locomotives appeared after this firm had become part of the North British Locomotive Company. These engines have been greatly under-rated, though many have said, with justification, that

30 One of Manson's two superheated 4-6-0s, with slight alterations by Whitelegg. A really excellent machine

there was no more handsome 4-6-0 ever produced in Britain. What has been overlooked is that these engines produced exactly the increase in power they were required to produce and in proportion to their increase in size. This was generally not true of 4-6-0s as compared with 4-4-0s in this country and it is worth observing that, though he was building a light, large engine to succeed a light, smaller one, Manson got some things right which more eminent engineers got wrong. In fact, the only other British 4-6-0 designer to get these things right, at the same moment in history, was Churchward. The main points of importance were the provision of valves on top of the outside cylinders, and the unequally divided coupled wheelbase which made it possible to fit a reasonably low grate and a capacious ashpan. The valves were of the balanced variety used on the inside cylinder engines, but proportional to their greater work. They were driven by a Stephenson link motion between the frames, which was what Churchward was doing at the same time. These engines had the first Belpaire fireboxes in Scotland. None of the original seventeen was ever superheated but Manson's last design was a superheated version of which two were built in 1911. There were some differences in the chassis, the cylinders being set slightly above the horizontal, fitted with piston valves. The whole front end layout was in fact altered and strengthened. The coal consumption of the saturated engines working 225 tons over the steep gradients of the Glasgow Carlisle section was a little over 50 lbs. per mile on average. Comparative trials with the superheated engines showed that they produced the customary economy of around 15%.

The Manson 4-6-0s were eventually displaced on the best duties by L.M.S. Midland compounds. There is no doubt that the G. & S.W. drivers came to appreciate the compounds and did superb work with them. There were only two superheated 4-6-0s, and in the L.M.S. mind, they were probably not distinguished from the seventeen saturated engines. It was only to be expected that a superheated compound 4-4-0, with a grate of over 28 sq. ft. would be a more potent machine than the old saturated 4-6-0. It was a common experience in Great Britain that superheated 4-4-0s were able to surpass saturated ten-wheelers which had been designed for a lower axle loading.

Peter Drummond's 4-4-0s repeated the story of his freight engines. Undoubtedly he was still under the influence of his brother who died at the time that the first Drummond 4-4-0s were being designed at Kilmarnock. The brilliance attributed to the Drummond

4-4-0s of the London & South Western was mostly extracted from them by the modifications of R. W. Urie. Peter Drummond brought most of his brother's principles, including much of the gimmickry, to the G. & S.W., but, as the younger man, he was able himself to embrace superheating and perhaps to cast off some of Dugald's ideas once Dugald's influence had been withdrawn. The fact is that the first of the Drummond G. & S.W. 4-4-0s were appalling machines, and they rolled frighteningly if they were ever allowed to run fast, which was only possible downhill. But these six were followed by another six with superheaters and with considerable changes in the details. Astonishingly, these later engines were amazingly economical and were fast and powerful, especially uphill. But the fact is that such heavy locomotives were not very suitable for the twisting routes of the railway, neither did they correspond to the temperaments of the enterprising G. & S.W. crews.

One last express locomotive must be mentioned and it is mentioned last because it was in a sense the last, though its origins went back to 1897. This was one of the most famous of all the engines of the railway, Manson's four cylinder 4-4-0. It was essentially one of his original design of large-wheeled express engines but arranged with four cylinders in line under the smokebox, their total volume approximating to that of the two cylinder variety. This engine produced no hammer blow and it was probably Manson's intention to get the civil engineers' agreement to an increase in axle loading to allow for this. But the civil engineers of the day were frequently unco-operative and Manson evidently did not achieve a satisfactory response, for he built no more four cylinder engines. But this engine, No. 11, was the first four cylinder simple expansion locomotive of normal type in these Islands and has been illustrated many times for this reason. It well shows the elegance of this designer's work but some of this elegance was lost when it received a larger boiler later in life. It became the last G. & S.W. express locomotive designed because R. H. Whitelegg used some parts of it in a total reconstruction which bore the name 'Lord Glenarthur'. This was also a four cylinder 4-4-0 but now there were only two valves, with cross-porting on each side. There was a large superheated boiler and the locomotive looked most impressive. In fact it did very well and fully justified the expense of the major reconstruction. It emerged from Kilmarnock Works on the 21st December 1922, just 10 days before the G. & S.W. ceased to exist, and it lasted for 12 years losing its old livery in exchange for L.M.S. red within a year or two.

Tank locomotives were long unpopular on the railway, especially for passenger work, but some were obviously essential for shunting. In addition to the 0-4-0 engines already mentioned, which were the heaviest of their kind in Britain, there were, of course, earlier and lighter engines of the same kind. Manson also produced a small batch of 0-6-0 tanks over a period of nearly twenty years around the turn of the century, but because the wheelbase of these was too long for some of the sharper curves encountered in industrial yards, he built six as 0-4-4 tanks, the trailing bogie having outside frames. These delightful locomotives were mainly used for shunting in the harbours at Ayr and Ardrossan, but inevitably were occasionally used for branch line passenger service. Earlier, Manson had built a small batch of larger 0-4-4 tanks for the Glasgow suburban services and these lasted for nearly forty years, though not for long on services for which they were designed because the railway made a practice of withdrawing suburban services as soon as competition from electric tramways made itself felt.

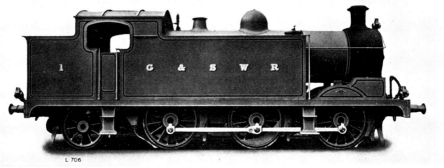

L 706

31 Peter Drummond's 0-6-2 tank

Years earlier, in James Stirling's time, a small group of locomotives with the same wheel arrangement had been built for working the Greenock Road. They were much disliked, mainly on account of the traditional prejudice of the railway and specific complaints were made that their water and fuel supplies were inadequate and that they had a tendency to roll on account of their high centre of gravity.

Against this background, it must be recorded that, in the last years of its independent existence, the railway owned two classes of tank locomotive which were universally acclaimed, entirely successful, and handsome in appearance. The first of these was the 0-6-2 tank designed by Peter Drummond, of which there were in the end twenty-eight. They were very similar to the same designer's 0-6-4 tanks for the Highland Railway and were used in freight and banking services. One of them was the last Glasgow & South Western engine to remain in main line service: it was withdrawn on the 17th April 1948, after thirty-nine years of work.

Lastly, we come to the six 4-6-4 or 'Baltic' tanks built in 1922 to the design of R. H. Whitelegg. Whitelegg had introduced this type of tank engine to Britain in 1912, when he was Locomotive Superintendent of the London, Tilbury & Southend Railway and he saw similarities between the heavy outer suburban services of that railway and those of the Glasgow & South Western. He therefore took the opportunity to build a bigger and better version of his Tilbury engines and the result was undoubtedly magnificent. He had had to make do and mend when dealing with the very run down post-War state of the G. & S.W. locomotives and he had made some sad mistakes in the process, but the Baltics were entirely his and he made few mistakes and those only in minor details in their design. Although there are insufficient test results or recorded performances to establish the point, there can be little doubt that these were the most powerful of all Scottish locomotives. They had 30 sq. ft. of grate, 22 in. × 26 in. cylinders, 6 ft. driving wheels and large superheaters. They were very beautifully finished and their designer had paid great attention to every aesthetic as well as to every technical detail. Their boilers were clad in unpainted blue steel which blended well with the light olive green of tanks, cab and bunker and was offset by the lining and the deep red of the footplate edging. There was much bright steel about them and they had the neat bunker top and fire iron racks on the tanks which Whitelegg had introduced on the Tilbury line.

Here then was an irony of history, because, while the great Caledonian Railway locomotive story petered out with heavy, sluggish, or complicated machines which were unworthy successors to the Caledonian tradition, the smaller rival railway produced a culminating triumph of locomotive engineering which aroused the admiration of the entire profession, of the travelling public, and of the men involved in operating them. But their splendour was short lived. There were only six of them and at the grouping Caledonian men took charge of the northern section of the L.M.S. Good, if pedestrian, standard types, made in large numbers, flooded the system, and the Baltic's day was done in a dozen years.

Unlike the Caledonian, the G.S.W.R. was formed by the amalgamation of two existing railway companies, the Glasgow, Paisley, Kilmarnock & Ayr and the Glasgow, Dumfries & Carlisle. Industrial activity around Glasgow and other manufacturing towns like Kilmarnock and Dumfries had early encouraged the development of canal and wagonway systems to ease the movement of goods to markets. The Kilmarnock & Troon line, later a part of the G.S.W.R., was in fact one of these early tramways, opened in 1811. The first major railway in the area was the Glasgow, Paisley, Kilmarnock & Ayr authorised in 1837 to tap the mineral wealth of Ayrshire. It was built through the Garnock valley via Prestwick, Troon, Kilwinning and Beith with a branch from Dalry to Kilmarnock. Opened in 1840, it had a tremendous effect on the canal trade from Ardrossan and Troon and on the tourist traffic from Glasgow to the coastal towns. By 1847 it had absorbed the Ardrossan & Johnstone line opened in 1837, bought the Paisley & Renfrew line also opened in 1837, and leased the Kilmarnock & Troon.

With the coastal towns so obviously benefiting from the advent of the railway, it was natural that attention should be turned to the possibility of continuing the line into England. The route considered was via the Nithsdale valley and in 1844 the Glasgow, Dumfries & Carlisle Railway was formed to promote the proposal against the rival Annandale scheme. The Nithsdale route would, it was argued, offer easier gradients and serve more large towns than the corresponding Annandale route and would link conveniently with the G.P.K. & A.R. when extended to Horsecleuch. Although there was much truth in the arguments, Parliament was only prepared to consider one line from England into Scotland and in 1845 decided in favour of the Annandale route and the Caledonian. The decision caused some confusion in the Glasgow, Dumfries & Carlisle ranks as to future strategy but in 1846 the company was reformed with plans for a line to run from the G.P.K. & A.R. at Horsecleuch (near Auchinleck) through the Nithsdale valley to join the Caledonian Railway near Gretna, so complying with the Parliamentary preference for but one route into Scotland. This proposal received Royal Assent in 1846. By 1850 the line was completed and the two companies concerned, the G.P.K. & A.R. and the G.D. & C., amalgamated to form the Glasgow & South Western Railway.

The development of the G.S.W.R. track network thereafter was concentrated on shortening the main routes, building branch lines to the mineral fields and coal fields of the area, and gaining access to the larger coastal ports for outlets to Ireland.

It was with this latter aim in view that the Ayr & Maybole and the Maybole & Girvan Railways were authorised to continue the G.S.W.R. line from Ayr to Girvan where a small packet station was to be established. The A. & M. was opened in 1856 and taken over by the G.S.W.R. in 1871 and the M. & G. opened in 1860 and amalgamated with the G.S.W.R. in 1865. The real aim of anyone attempting to exploit the Irish traffic however was to reach Portpatrick, at this time a declining little port south of Stranraer. In the event

it proved totally unsuitable as a steamer terminal and the main services had to be transfered to Stranraer, but during the 1850s and 60s it was the undoubted goal of a number of railway companies. The Ayr & Girvan reached there in 1877, when the Girvan & Portpatrick Junction Railway, first authorised in 1865 and again in 1870, was finally opened; but by this time the steamer services on the Clyde had become established and there was little traffic for the new line. By 1886 the company, in grave financial difficulties, was dissolved and reformed as the Ayrshire & Wigtownshire, and it was this company which was absorbed by the G.S.W.R. in 1892.

From the East, a line was built to Portpatrick via Dumfries and Castle Douglas and opened in two stages by independent companies. The first stage was built by the Castle Douglas & Dumfries Company and opened in 1859. This was later extended to Kirkcud-bright and both sections amalgamated with the G.S.W.R. in 1865. The second stage from Castle Douglas to Portpatrick was built by the Portpatrick Company authorised in 1857 and opened throughout in 1862. The importance of this line commanding the shortest sea route to Ireland can be seen from the fact that initially it was worked by the L.N.W.R. and the Caledonian. After 1885, when it amalgamated with the Wigtownshire Railway running from Newton Stewart to Whithorn, the G.S.W.R. and the Midland joined those responsible for working the line.

Further north the G.S.W.R. was concentrating on gaining access to the coastal and Clyde ports. The Caledonian had the early advantage on the Clyde with its port at Greenock but in 1865, the G.S.W.R. saw its opportunity to rival the Caley by supporting the Greenock & Ayrshire Railway planned to run from Princes Pier at Greenock to Bridge of Weir, where it would join the G.S.W.R. branch line from Johnstone. Coal and mineral traffic would be the main staple of the new line, augmented by substantial receipts from steamboat passengers. The line was opened in 1869 and keen competition commenced with the Caledonian. With Princes Pier better placed for the interchange of traffic from boat to train, the G.S.W.R. had a certain advantage over the Caley which it exploited to the full, and by 1871 it had become the favourite route to the coast. Steamers ran to Liverpool, Fleetwood and Ardrossan and at the weekends traffic to and from Glasgow was particularly heavy. The freight traffic, however, never reached the levels expected. A new G.S.W.R. station was built at Princes Pier in 1894. This was prompted by a new Caledonian pier at Gourock. Thereafter, honours were even, but rivalry was even fiercer.

Almost concurrently, the G.S.W.R. was losing custom to the Caledonian at Ardrossan, the main port of the company on the Ayrshire coast. The Caledonian's new line to the port coupled with the introduction of its fine new steamer, the 'Duchess of Hamilton', was proving too much for the G.S.W.R. which had hitherto relied on private steam packet companies for its services to Ireland and the Scottish Islands. To regain its pre-eminence the Sou' West fought and won the legal battle to run its own steamers from the port and in 1892 introduced a large, fast, 2 funnelled steamer, the 'Glen Sannox', which fully matched the rival 'Duchess of Hamilton'.

In June 1882, a new line was opened to Fairlie Pier, north of Ardrossan, whence steamers were run to Campbeltown, and in 1885 this line was extended to Largs whence steamers ran to Millport.

To shorten the main line and improve services to Glasgow, a joint G.S.W.R.–Caledonian line had been built in 1873, running from Glasgow via Barrhead and Stewarton to Kilmarnock. This greatly facilitated the new Anglo-Scottish service which followed the opening of the Midland railway's Settle & Carlisle line. In Glasgow itself, business for the railway was brisk and relations with the neighbouring Edinburgh & Glasgow line were good, the only problem between the two being their lack of physical connection. It was not unknown, when rivalry with the 'Caley' was at its height, for the G.S.W.R. to route its freight consignments via Gretna to reach the E. & G.R. on the opposite side of the Clyde, rather than send them over Caley metals. To overcome this problem, the E. & G.R. and the G.S.W.R. promoted the City of Glasgow Union Railway to build a line 6¼ miles long, bridging the Clyde. In the event, it proved a very difficult line to build, taking 11 years to complete, but it was finally opened in 1876 together with the magnificent new station at St. Enoch. The station and approaches were taken over by the G.S.W.R. in 1883 and St. Enoch then became the headquarters of the company.

As far as branch lines were concerned, a line to the Dalmellington ironworks was opened in 1856 and absorbed by the G.S.W.R. in 1858. Under the Light Railways Act of 1896, the company built a line up the thinly populated coast between Ayr and Girvan and another up to the Cairn valley to Moniaive, and in 1903 built a branch to Catrine to serve the cotton industry.

The early coaching stock of the G.S.W.R. (then the G.P.K. & A.R.) was as primitive as that on any other line. The carriages were 4 wheeled vehicles, with three compartments in the 1st class and open trucks for the 3rd class passengers. Like most other companies, the South West bought much of its early stock from outside contractors and it was not until Patrick Stirling was engineer (1853-1866) that the company began to make its own 4 wheeled coaches. The locomotive and carriage works were moved from Glasgow to Kilmarnock in 1856. James Stirling, Patrick's successor, introduced the company's first 6 wheeled stock in which the compartment divisions were extended to the roof. Corridor stock was introduced in 1899 when a complete set of coaches was built for the Glasgow to Stranraer boat train. By 1890 when James Manson became locomotive engineer, the works at Kilmarnock were becoming cramped and overcrowded. In 1901, therefore, the carriage and wagon section was transferred to Barassie, although Kilmarnock was kept open for locomotive work. Among the outstanding coaches built at Barassie were some 70 ft. non-corridor twelve-wheeled bogies, fitted with electric light and steam heating.

By the 20th century the G.S.W.R. had established a large weekend commuter traffic between Glasgow and the Islands, in addition to its important Anglo-Scottish services, its seasonal holiday traffic and its by no means negligible goods trade amounting in 1910 to 7 million tons of minerals and 1½ million tons of other merchandise. It had amply fulfilled the hopes of the early promoters who had designed the coat of arms linking symbolically, townships, craft industries and the sea ports.

Major Routes of the Highland Railway

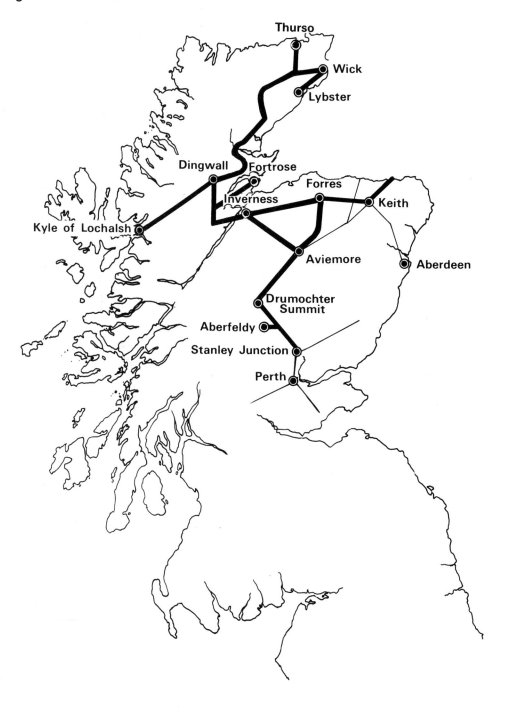

thin lines indicate other connecting railways

The Highland Railway

33 Highland 2-4-0 with large snow plough

No British railway had a more romantic name than the Highland. The image of the Highlands is one of remote beauty and that of the Highlander one of strength and solitariness and of a good way of life, but little touched by luxury. To this must be added the romantic colour, the bright tartans and the music of the pipes. The reality of Highland life is not so different from the popular image but, to those that live in more populous regions, it is hard to realise what, in practice, living in a sparsely populated landscape is like, or to comprehend how hard a Highland winter might be, especially because the tourist of to-day usually visits the far north only in summer.

The Highland Railway was inevitably true to its geographical setting and the economics of the area it served. Except for an extraordinary period in the 1914-1918 War, when it carried vast quantities of men, munitions and fuel destined for the great Naval base at Scapa Flow, the Highland was not a transit line through which traffic flowed between major centres, as is the case with some remote and mountainous main lines in Europe and elsewhere. Its routes served its own territory and not much else, though part of that territory lay on the islands off the northern coasts. Almost all the route mileage was single track and, although great ingenuity had been exercised in choosing the routes which were easier to build and not too difficult to operate, the highest point on any British main line was to be found at Drumochter, right in the middle of Northern Scotland on the route from Stanley Junction, north of Perth, to Aviemore where the line to Inverness parted from that to Forres. The height of the summit was, and is, 1,484 ft., and though this may not seem any great altitude by comparison with other railway summits around the world, the gradients approaching it are still formidable, involving long stretches at 1 in 80 and portions even steeper. Also, although a firm footing might be expected for railway tracks

34 Stroudley's famous shunting tank, the prototype of the 'Terriers'

in mountainous country, there was much treacherous ground to be covered, such as near Dava Moor where, even after extensive excavations and re-making of the foundation, the rails could be observed to move up and down 3 ins. or 4 ins. as trains passed over. Only repeated re-ballasting over a period of years finally consolidated the soil.

Mention has already been made, in the introduction to this book, of the appalling conditions that can be produced by heavy snow falls. Although all the Scottish railways suffered more or less, the Highland was undoubtedly far worse affected than the others and it was the regular practice to fit snow ploughs to locomotives working from some depots, attachments which could only be removed during the summer months. There were several sizes of these, matched to the difficulty of the route and to the power of the locomotive. In view of the severity of weather conditions it is perhaps remarkable that the Highland never provided much protection for its locomotive crews, but it may be that the character of these men would have been opposed to greater comfort. Certainly, it is strange to contrast the cab of a North Eastern locomotive of the 1880s with the equivalent provision on any Scottish railway but the Highland seemed even less concerned to keep out the wind than did the others.

The name of the Highland Railway dates from 1865 but its origins go back ten years earlier. It is an unfortunate but frequently observed fact that innovation takes time to travel and so one need not be surprised that the earlier locomotives of the Highland Railway were already old fashioned when they were new. This, of course, has also something to do with wealth and, though the remoter and less prosperous railways did not actually buy their equipment secondhand as a rule, they frequently had to make do with people who had not achieved the greatest success when they had been in greater centres of activity. Such a man was Alexander Allan. He had been very much at the centre of affairs as Works Manager at Crewe and the 'Crewe' type of locomotive, in which the outside cylinders are sandwiched between inner and outer frames and drive on to wheels carried by the inner frames only, is commonly associated with his name. This is not the place to

35 Another tiny Highland tank, 'Highlander'

investigate his claims to have originated it: suffice it that he did not make these claims until those who could have contradicted them with authority were dead, and historians have not agreed since on the precise nature of Allan's contribution. One thing which was undoubtedly his, and undoubtedly excellent also, was the straight link valve gear which became so widespread and probably contributed to the excellence of the L. & N.W.R. 2-4-0s.

Allan himself drifted away from the centre of things and became Engineer of the Scottish Central Railway and of the Inverness & Nairn, the original component of the Highland. Allan's influence in Scotland was great and the 'Crewe' design spread from the Scottish Central to the Caledonian, to which, surprisingly, Allan did not become Locomotive Engineer when the Scottish Central was absorbed. However Benjamin Conner developed the type with great success until his retirement in 1876. On the Highland Railway, the great exponent of the 'Crewe' design was David Jones, who only forsook it near the end of his career with his celebrated 'Big Goods' of 1894. But before Jones took over in 1869 there was a short period in which the first Highland Locomotive Engineer held office, and this was the eminent William Stroudley. Stroudley was an Englishman from Oxfordshire, but he had worked on the Edinburgh & Glasgow Railway, where he had almost certainly been responsible for at least one locomotive design, though not nominally in charge. Stroudley was a perfectionist and spent his few years with the Highland mainly in improving the material which the new company had inherited from its various constituents, and also in improving beyond recognition the Lochgorm Works, by Inverness. His only new design for the Railway was a small 0-6-0 shunting tank locomotive, generally recognised as the predecessor of his famous 'Terriers' on the London, Brighton & South Coast. The Stroudley cab made its appearance on re-built 'Crewe' type locomotives, in much the same form as it was later to appear on the 'Gladstones', and the 'Improved Engine Green' or greenish-yellow livery was another characteristic he left behind when he went south.

It was undoubtedly David Jones who gave much of its individual character to the Highland Railway. He was, in fact, more than a locomotive engineer and his influence on the whole system was considerable. Of his locomotives, the most individual was a long series of 4-4-0s with sloping outside cylinders embraced within the curve of the smokebox

36 A Jones 'Skye Bogie' at Inverness

wrapper, as on the Stirling 8 footers and the older Crewe engines. The 'Crewe' type of framing was here applied to an engine with a leading bogie and the bold curves of that front end, though slightly cumbersome, at speed suggested the bow-wave of a ship; and a slightly marine touch was also added by the fat parallel Jones chimney which had louvres in the front. Unfortunately, the whistle was not fixed to the upper front of the chimney to complete the steamer effect, but was usually fixed by the safety valves in the normal place. These 4-4-0s had evolved from 2-4-0s of the 'Crewe Goods' type. Jones himself built nothing but bogie engines, the first 4-4-0s appearing in 1874, just after some similar re-builds of the older machines. These large wheeled engines, the 'Dukes', were followed some years later by the smaller wheeled 'Skye Bogies' named because of their service on the long branch from Dingwall to Kyle of Lochalsh. The trains along this route traversed beautiful but rather desolate sheep farming country, which they served with all the necessities of life, and the same is true even to-day, because in such sparsely populated regions the railway remains the centre of the way of life and also an important employer. One would not lightly undertake the long drive from, say, Achanalt to Inverness except in beautiful weather. The Skye Bogies remained in service on this line for some fifty years, working passengers and goods, a holiday line for some in summer, but a lifeline for all in winter.

In 1894 Jones produced the locomotive to which he most owes his place in railway history: the 'Jones Goods'. This was the first 4-6-0 design for a British main line railway, and it departed from his previous practice in the final abandonment of 'Crewe' type framing which had become unnecessary with the availability of more reliable materials. His last 4-4-0s, the 'Loch' class, also followed the simpler, modern construction, but, although these locomotives first built in 1896 were repeated as late as 1917, it is the 'Big Goods' which deserves our greater attention. These engines had driving wheels of the size used in most 0-6-0 goods engines, but instead of the usual inside arrangement of the cylinders Jones, sticking to his preferences, provided a leading bogie and outside cylinders. This long engine had a proportionately large boiler and was in fact the largest locomotive type in the British Isles: a remarkable thing to appear on the northern-most

37 The earliest Jones express 4-4-0

38 The famous 'Jones Goods'

railway. The design was strong and straightforward and it has been suggested that it was inspired by current locomotive construction in Scotland for overseas, especially for India. But it is equally likely that this overseas construction was itself influenced by David Jones, because he acted as consultant to overseas railways in their dealings with the Scottish locomotive manufacturers.

The basic design of the 'Jones Goods' was to be followed, on the Highland Railway, in that of the 'Castles' which had driving wheels of the mixed traffic diameter of 5 ft. 9 ins., but which were essentially express locomotives. The same style appeared on the Great Central, the North Eastern and eventually even on the Caledonian, while on the Glasgow & South Western, James Manson modified it in ways which were also applied to the later deliveries for India. Without any doubt, this was one of the landmarks in British locomotive history.

The 'Castles' were nominally a design of Peter Drummond, but in fact he found the design complete when he succeeded Jones in 1896. Though he perpetuated the Jones 4-6-0s his own contribution took the form of locomotives very like those which his brother was building on the London & South Western: large and small 4-4-0s with inside cylinders (known as the large and small 'Bens'), conventional 0-6-0s, and a variety of tank engines of which the largest and most interesting was the 0-6-4 design used for banking at Drumochter. These engines, first built in 1909, all had long lives. They were both handsome and effective and when Drummond left the Highland for the 'Sou' West' in 1911, he built some generally similar 0-6-2 tanks for the latter railway.

In fact, the Highland Railway had an interesting variety of tank engines, many of them very small. Drummond built some 0-4-4s which worked the Strathpeffer branch, where

39 A 'Castle' at Perth. Jones design with Drummond features

they succeeded some much older engines: 0-4-4 saddle tanks, 0-4-2s and 2-4-0s. There were some older 0-4-4 side tanks, mainly associated with the branch from Wick to Lybster, but perhaps the best known of David Jones' tank engines was one which did not belong to the Highland Railway at all. This was the Duke of Sutherland's private engine 'Dunrobin', a 0-4-4 tank built to replace a much older and rather primitive machine which was bought off the Duke by the Highland Railway and re-built as a charming 2-4-0 named 'Gordon Castle.' 'Dunrobin' was little used on the Duke of Sutherland's private railway, on which its train in later days consisted of the bogie saloon now at the National Railway Museum in York, and the four wheeled small saloon which, in later years, was relegated to the task of steadying the tail of the big one. The locomotive and both saloons have fortunately survived, 'Dunrobin' and the small saloon now being in Canada. The engine had an especially capacious cab with a seat across the back above the coal bunker for the Duke's guests. The signatures of those guests, including several crowned heads and many other notables, were to be found written all over the inside of the rear spectacle plate.

The last locomotive engineer of the Highland Railway was Christopher Cumming but between his advent and the resignation of Drummond there were some three years in which F. G. Smith looked after the locomotive affairs. Smith perpetuated the 'Castle' 4-6-0s but his main contribution to Scottish locomotive history was in the creation of an entirely new and modern style of locomotive design which, unfortunately for him, resulted in his enforced resignation. He designed a large modern 4-6-0 without adequately consulting the Civil Engineer. There was even a hint of secrecy about the way the locomotive was designed because the drawings were produced in the drawing office of the North British Railway so the Highland engineers could not have had a sight of them or even heard rumours of what was being proposed. Six engines were built to these drawings and very fine engines they were. With Belpaire boilers, large piston valves above the cylinders operated by Walschaert's valve gear, good valve timing, and high running plates, they looked completely modern and very handsome. But the Civil Engineer would have none of them and they were all sold, at a considerable profit, to the Caledonian Railway immediately, while Smith left the service of the Railway and pursued a successful career elsewhere. On the Caledonian these engines proved to be the best of all 4-6-0s on that railway.

40 Drummond 'Small Ben' 4-4-0 at Achterneed on a train for Kyle, in L.M.S. days. L.M.S. red suited Highland engines very well

But though Smith had gone his style was destined to stay. He had designed two modern 4-4-0s, 'Snaigow' and 'Durn' for working on the northern-most section to Wick. These were the only British two cylinder 4-4-0s with external Walschaert's valve gear and compared in appearance with the much later Gresley 'Shire' and the Southern 'School'. They were built by Hawthorn, Leslie and Co., who built the 4-6-0s, and, on Christopher Cumming's instructions, the same builders built a closely similar small wheeled 4-6-0—a modern version of the Jones Goods. These, too, were most powerful and efficient machines. A passenger version followed later, the 'Clan' of which eight were built between 1919 and 1921, the last engines built for the Highland Railway. These later 4-6-0s were also built by Hawthorn, Leslie and it is difficult to say whether they owed most to their builders, to Cumming, or to Smith.

The carriages of the Highland Railway in the later years of its existence were unremarkable. There was a predominance of shortish bogie coaches with almost flat sides and low arc roofs. Many of these had vertical planking conspicuous on their sides. The predominant livery was dark green and they were almost all gas lit. The appearance was plain, decent, and frugal. A little earlier some of these vehicles had been painted in a two-tone livery with the light upper panels which were once so favoured in the British Isles.

Highland carriages in the 19th century were, however, much more amusing and varied and included one or two considerable innovations. David Jones was responsible for the first side-corridor sleeping compartment carriages in Britain, though there were imported Pullman sleepers with the characteristic and different Pullman arrangement of berths. There were three of the Highland sleeping cars and full details are hard to come by, but

41 Probably the best of the Scottish 4-6-0s, one of F. G. Smith's Highland 'Rivers' in Caledonian ownership, at Perth

the principal historian of the Railway has recorded that there were single berth compartments at the ends, a four berth men's compartment with a two tier arrangement, and a three berth women's compartment, all berths being at a normal, single, level. The side corridor appears to have given access to separate men's and women's toilet facilities. This was in 1878, before the days of vestibule connection between coaches, and there would certainly have been an attendants' compartment included in the coach. Jones was also responsible for some unusual looking six wheeled carriages which were described as 'chariot ended'. These ends were slightly bowed and provided with windows: they contained a single sided or coupe compartment, the occupants of which were thus provided with a particularly good view if their carriage was marshalled at the end of the train. And on the Highland Railway the views thus opened up could be romantic indeed. The shape of these ends was decidedly ornamental, the ends of the sides being turned out towards the buffer beam to allow for the bowed glazed portion. There were ordinary compartments in the middle of the coach. Although most were six wheelers there was an eight wheeled design. The effect when two were marshalled together might have been slightly bizarre, as the occupants of adjacent coupes would sit looking at each other through a double glass barrier which prevented the occasional scrap of conversation by which strangers facing each other in ordinary compartments could break the ice.

Among the four wheeled stock there were some quaint survivors of a distant past which long survived on remoter branch lines such as those to Lybster, Strathpeffer or Aberfeldy. Some of these had windows with rounded tops and what biologists would call an exo-skeleton—the framing of the coach was lined on the inside but not clad on the outside.

The stations of the Highland Railway were not designed to encourage the traveller to linger. On the other hand, from a railway operating point of view, many held the interest of being passing points on single track lines. Here stopping trains would exchange their tablets (the physical token of the possession of a stretch of railway), by hand. Non-stopping trains might do this also and the locomotive firemen and the signalmen developed specially robust arms as a result of the exchanging of tablets en passant. Some had pads and

42 Strathpeffer branch train at Dingwall. The locomotive is one of two originally built for export to Uruguay. The Highland bought them and three new ones as well

leather patches on their sleeves, the tablets being contained in pouches with large loops attached which could be caught on outstretched arms. But, after James Manson, during his period on the Great North of Scotland, had invented a satisfactory mechanical tablet exchanger (which he did not patent in order that its use should not be restricted and that its benefits should therefore be felt by the servants of all railway companies which could use it), the Manson apparatus was attached to almost all Highland locomotives and the corresponding ground apparatus appeared in very many Highland stations. Most Highland station buildings were of wood—examples of that comely, pavilion-like, type of design which resulted from the factory-made components of the system. But, where the building was of sufficient importance to justify the expense, or where the weather conditions were likely to be exceptionally severe even by Highland standards, solid stone structures appeared. Experiments were also made with snow screens on some stretches of line, and there was even one structure designed to stop the prevailing wind from engulfing the railway track in sand.

One might perhaps conclude reference to the look of the Highland Railway with the description of a couple of representative trains. In spite of the larger and more modern locomotives of the last years, the most typical Highland 'big' engine was a 'Castle'. A curious quirk of history resulted in fifty of these engines being built for the Western Railway of France, at a time when the European locomotive building industry was overloaded with orders and this happened to be the type which the Scottish builders could produce most quickly, ironically just when five British railways were having to buy locomotives from the United States of America. The French 'Castle' looked exactly like the Highland one but was usually used for much less dignified services.

The Highland 'Castle' would be dark green. It would usually be puffing hard and proceeding briskly on a train of mixed make-up with mainly dark green short bogie coaches but with one or two disproportionately larger and handsomer vehicles in that dark brown and cream livery which, though variously described, was more or less common to the London & North Western and Caledonian Railways. This train might well be bringing sportsmen from the south and there might be a number of four wheeled vans of various types, possibly with horses, very probably with dogs and guns, and certainly with mails. This train would look brisk and business-like and almost opulent but to the eyes of those accustomed to the great railways further south, there would be some incongruity in the fact that it was travelling on a single track. The other train of which we might evoke the memory would have a Jones 'Skye bogie' on the front and would be one of those mixed trains which used to keep remote places between Dingwall and Kyle in touch with civilisation. This train looked, and very largely was, antique. The tall louvred chimney and sweeping curves of the engine's front end now, standing at a station, suggested some mobile portion of a Victorian drawing room. What was behind the engine suggested more the potting shed .than the drawing room but it must be said that the doors of mid-Victorian four wheeled carriages were usually thick and shut with a solid sound which suggested that the potting shed was made to last. But the important part of the train was the part in which the mails and the assorted light freight were carried. The essential supplies of cast iron pipes, glazed sinks, paper, cotton goods, whisky and innumerable other commodities which were awaited with patience, or even with enthusiasm: these were the blessings which the old but excellent Jones engine brought to the Highlands along the single track railway.

Running from Inverness to Wick and Thurso in the north and from Inverness to Stanley Junction, just outside Perth, in the south, the Highland Railway was conceived and built as a lifeline for the Highland capital and the other centres of population in the far north of Scotland.

There was talk of a railway to serve the Highlands of Scotland as early as 1840 when various schemes were put forward for linking Inverness to Aberdeen or Perth. The burghers of Inverness, quite naturally, favoured the more direct route south via Perth, but in the contest which followed it was the Great North of Scotland Railway that triumphed with its plans for the Aberdeen to Inverness line. The near financial collapse of the G.N. of S., however, gave the Inverness party another opportunity of achieving its aims. This time their proposal came in stages, commencing with a short line from Inverness to Nairn which blocked the Great North's advance and also began the route to Perth. The line was opened in November 1855 and plans were at once made for extending it to Elgin to join the G.N. of S. In view of the latter's desperate financial situation another company, the Inverness & Aberdeen Junction Railway, was granted permission to extend the line right through from Nairn to Keith. This section was opened in 1858 and was amalgamated with the Inverness and Nairn line in 1861.

At first the G.N. of S. was represented on the board of the Inverness & Aberdeen Junction Railway but as suspicions began to grow that the company was planning an independent route to Inverness, their representatives were forced to leave the councils of the I.A.J.R. This left the way open for a revival of the Perth scheme. The Inverness & Perth Junction Railway was authorised in 1861 and the line, branching from Forres and running to Dunkeld via Dava and Dalwhinnie, was opened in 1863. It traversed some wild countryside before joining the Perth & Dunkeld Railway built in 1856. Dava Moor, for instance, 1,052 feet above sea level, was notorious for its deep snows in winter and it was only with difficulty that the Highland managed to work the line continuously.

43 The Duke of Sutherland's train

Meanwhile to the north of Inverness major landowners were planning extensions to the railway to serve their sheep farming interest and the local centres of population. Sir Alexander Matheson of Ardross, chairman of the Highland Railway from its foundation in 1865, was determined to have a line from Inverness to Wick and Thurso, but following early experiences with the Perth line, he decided to approach the problem piecemeal. The first section from Inverness to Invergordon was authorised in 1860 to run via Beauly and Dingwall. It was known as the Ross-shire Railway until its amalgamation with the Inverness & Aberdeen Junction line in 1862 and it was opened throughout in 1863. Even before this however Matheson, together with the Duke of Sutherland, eager to secure rail links for his estates, was planning extensions to the line. The Duke contributed a substantial sum of money to the new line on the understanding that it would go onto Bonar Bridge instead of terminating at Tain; so the Ross-shire extension act was passed in 1863 and the line opened to Bonar Bridge in 1864.

There were by this time two major rail companies working closely together in the Highlands, the Inverness & Aberdeen Junction and the Inverness & Perth Junction, and in 1865 they amalgamated to form the Highland Railway. The continuation of the Ross-shire Railway, northwards from Bonar Bridge, although worked by the Highland, remained an independent company until 1884. The Duke of Sutherland was again foremost in promoting this continuation of the line to fulfill his ideal of linking the major centres of population with Inverness. To achieve this he had to sacrifice the easiest, most direct route north in order to take the line via the towns of Lairg, Rogart and Golspie. The Sutherland Railway Company formed to build the line had found the engineering work involved so heavy and so expensive that by 1868 they were no further than Golspie and the Duke himself had to step in with money and plans for his own railway from Golspie to Helmsdale. Construction work had already begun by the time the plan was authorised in 1870 and the line was opened the following year.

There was then just 30 miles separating the Highland trains at Helmsdale from Wick on the northeast coast of Scotland, but when plans were considered for completing the link, the towns of Caithness put forward a strong case for inclusion in any rail communication proposals. The Sutherland & Caithness Railway, authorised in 1871, incorporated the views of these major towns in taking the line via Forsinard, with a branch from Georgemas Junction to Thurso. The line was opened in 1874 and covered some 60 miles between Helmsdale and Wick.

Up in the very north of Scotland, there was no competition for traffic, only bleak conditions and challenging snow drifts, against which William Stroudley, the locomotive engineer, had designed a large wedge shaped plough almost the height of the engine. In 1874, when the new line opened, it took an average of 7 hours 15 minutes to travel between Inverness and Wick in old style four wheeled coaches with no corridors, no conveniences and no food, the only appreciable stops being at Tain and Bonar Bridge. Such was the character and the spirit of the Highland Railway.

The Highland's outlet to the western isles came through the Dingwall & Skye Railway's proposal for a line terminating at Kyle of Lochalsh opposite Kyleakin. The company was backed financially by both the Caledonian and the Highland and the line was authorised in 1865. One of the few instances of local opposition met with by the Highland in its rail building programmes occurred during the building of this line when Sir William Mackenzie refused to have the railway in the town of Strathpeffer. The inhabitants of Strathpeffer were later to regret his decision but in deference to his views the Dingwall & Skye line passed over the rocky hills to the north of the town before descending to Garve and Achnasheen. Instead of taking the line right through to Kyle of Lochalsh as originally intended, the Dingwall & Skye stopped short at Strome Ferry and established its ferry terminal and pier for landing sheep and cattle. It was opened in 1870 and worked by the Highland Railway until its full absorption in 1880. Packet steamships were operated by the Dingwall & Skye from 1870 but not very successfully and in 1877 they sold their ships to the Highland. They did little better however and by 1880 all the steamship interests at Strome Ferry were handed over to the famous David MacBrayne.

Opposition to the Railway in Strathpeffer had died away by 1885 and a branch line was opened to serve the town, but it was never as convenient as direct communication would have been. The final extension to the Dingwall & Skye line was in 1897 when the North British ambitions for opening up the western highlands prompted the Highland Railway to complete its connection to Kyle of Lochalsh. The line proved difficult and expensive to build but once opened it offered much improved facilities for transfer between boat and train than ever existed at Strome Ferry.

On the Eastern front relations with the G. N. of S. were far from friendly and both railways battled to gain the upper hand. In 1862 the Highland constructed a branch line from Alves to Burghead in the hope of sealing off the Great North's advance along the coast to Findhorn and in 1884 opened another branch to Buckie and Portessie to gain an independent access to the coast and the important fishing ports. To counter proposals backed by the Great North for a line from Boat of Garten to Inverness the Highland proposed and built its own direct line from Inverness to Aviemore. The line was authorised in 1884. It was very expensive to build and to run and it by-passed the major centres of population. It was of course much faster than the older route but quite probably it would never have been built had it not been for the ambitions of the Great North of Scotland Railway.

Two more branch lines were built on the eastern front in 1893, to Hopeman and to Fochabers. In 1894 the Black Isle branch was opened from Muir of Ord to Fortrose and under the Light Railways Act of 1896, the line from the Mound to Dornoch was opened in 1902.

At times the Highland Railway could appear as unco-operative and brusque as the G.N. of S. in its dealings with other companies, but the explanation lies in the inception of the company. It was from its beginnings more of a local line than a trunk route, built by the

Highlanders for the Highlanders. At first there was little concern on the Highland board for developing tourist traffic. The prime function of the railway was the transportation of goods and cattle southwards from Inverness and Sutherland. Nevertheless, the tourist potential was there and was developed on a reasonable scale during the 1880s and 90s. At Kyle of Lochalsh, where tourists could be expected for Skye and Stornoway, the Highland bought Kyle House just above the ferry terminus and ran it as a pleasant hotel. The Strathpeffer Spa Express was introduced in an attempt to popularise this district as a tourist resort. There were of course, regular connections for the London sleeping cars from both Euston and Kings Cross although at one stage the Highland, being anxious to keep the train loads to a minimum, refused to pull any 'foreign' sleeping cars not adequately patronised.

Following the race to the north of 1895, the Highland began widening the Blair-Atholl, Dalwhinnie section of its track in anticipation of an increased influx of traffic, but in the event the traffic receipts hardly justified the cost of the work. Nevertheless under the General Managership of Andrew Dougall, who served the Highland from 1855 until forced to resign under suspicion of financial dishonesty in 1895, the company had flourished financially reaching a new level of prosperity in 1892.

The early years of the 20th century saw much re-equipment of the system, but though the quality of everything was sound, the quantity of motive power and rolling stock was kept to the minimum required to work the summer season's traffic. During this period everything was at work, and the vital maintenance was deferred until winter. This worked well enough until 1914, but then the heavy wartime traffic took no account of seasons. The Highland was able to keep going only by borrowing locomotives and stock from other railways—and this was, obviously, selected by those railways as being most readily spared, and so less useful to the Highland than might have been hoped for. But the railway did wonderful work and received public thanks for its amazing contribution to the national effort, the way it had handled the huge traffic for which it had never been designed or equipped. And after 1918 it just had time to start the process of renewal and recovery before it was absorbed—but did not lose its identity—in the L.M.S.

Major routes of the Great North of Scotland Railway

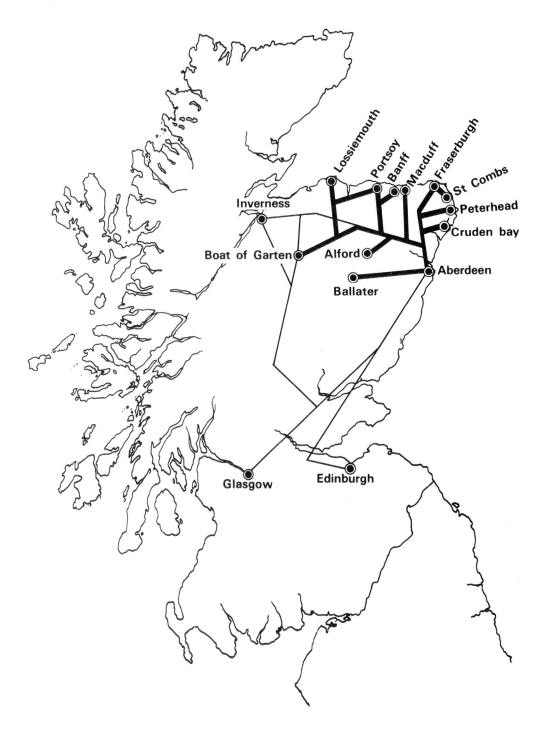

thin lines indicate other connecting railways

The Great North of Scotland Railway

44 Royal train on the Great North of Scotland

The tradition has grown up that there were sixteen major Pre-Grouping railways, and one of these was the Great North of Scotland. This small but interesting system was featured in 'Our Home Railways', by W. J. Gordon, an earlier publication similar to the present one. Gordon added the London Underground and one other railway to the sixteen, but, as his two volume work first appeared in 1910, the concept of a Pre-Grouping railway did not yet exist. In 1944 Colonel Rixon Bucknall produced the first version of his small but enjoyable historical survey, 'Our Railway History', and in this, too, the Great North of Scotland has its place.

It is not in any carping spirit that the present author implies a question mark over the status of this interesting and well conducted small railway. The reason for this introduction is really to make it plain that this was, in fact, a small railway, and only the fact of its being in a particular corner of Scotland gives it a cachet which previous historians have denied to other systems of similar size. The Great North of Scotland was not more considerable than the Cambrian, with which it had substantial affinities. It was, in fact, more or less in the Cambrian's class. A busier and more prosperous system was the Taff Vale, and there were railways like the Furness, the North Staffordshire and the London, Tilbury & Southend which were of equal importance and interest. Yet the Great North of Scotland has acquired the status of a major Pre-Grouping railway and it is worth trying to analyse why.

One reason immediately springs to mind: this railway regularly saw Royal trains to Ballater, for Balmoral. There were no doubt Royal trains on the Cambrian, but anything of this kind on the admirable North Staffordshire or the extremely prosperous and profitable Taff Vale was quite exceptional. Another thing which lent a particular character to the Great North of Scotland was the fact that for many years it used nothing but 4-4-0 tender locomotives for all its services. Then, again, there was its legendary rivalry with and hostility to the Highland and the struggles for domination around Aberdeen. Possibly this small railway has earned the attention of history because it was a symbol of Scottish independence taken to the point of truculence.

The fact is that in its earlier years the Great North of Scotland was as thoroughly awkward as any railway could be. In Aberdeen, which was the centre (though not geogra-

45 G.N.S.R. 2-4-0, No. 7

phically so) of its operations, it long had a relationship of mutual hatred with the Caledonian. When the two railways had separate stations, and a bus was provided to enable Caledonian passengers to transfer to the G.N.S., the platform barrier would be closed in the passengers' faces and the little train would puff off northwards without them. There was endless argument and legal wrangling between the two companies until the G.N.S. 'grew up'. It was possibly galling for the smaller company to see all that fish from the Aberdeen trawlers, which it regarded as providing its own natural traffic, pass southwards on the tracks of its great rival instead of being taken more circuitously but more profitably across to the Highland Railway.

But with the Highland Railway, relations were even worse. Whereas eventually a joint station was established at Aberdeen, the Great North never succeeded in effecting an entry into Inverness over its own tracks. It long attempted to secure an Act enabling it to build such a line, but the Highland successfully resisted it and for many years the G.N.S. was obliged to hand over its traffic from Aberdeen at Elgin, which lies roughly halfway between the two major towns. In fact, the Great North was nearer to Inverness, but to the south east, at Boat of Garten; but the connections from that point on the Highland Railway tended southwards through Aviemore. The Great North 'grew up' as a result of having to endure the consequences of its own attitudes, which included the building of new lines of railway, such as the completion of the connection between Perth and Inverness, which might not have been necessary had the smaller railway been more co-operative. Once the Great North had achieved maturity there was even a suggestion of amalgamation with the Highland but, the latter railway developing 'cold feet' at a late stage, closer working agreements were agreed in substitution and the trains of the smaller railway began to be hauled by their own locomotives right into Inverness, while Highland locomotives pulled their trains right into Aberdeen.

Like the Highland, this railway is mostly single track. In fact little more than one-sixth of its 300 odd route miles are doubled. There are no particularly striking engineering works along the line, though the bridge over the Spey is an impressive structure. There are also no great summits or very long or steep gradients. The railway was, even, less afflicted by the weather than the other Scottish lines and seemed to go about its business with a quiet serenity which concealed the ambitions and the struggles of its Board of Directors.

46 A long-lived Cowan 4-4-0

Visually one could almost imagine that this railway set out to show just how pleasing a train could look. For many years its carriages were a darkish red below the waistline and white above it, and its engines were green. Around the turn of the century, some engines of Great North of Scotland design were sold by the makers to the South Eastern & Chatham Railway, and there their particular lineaments inspired the design of Harry Wainwright's class D 4-4-0s, which are regarded by many as the ultimate expression of British locomotive elegance. But few of those who admire No. 737 in the National Railway Museum at York are aware that the inspiration of this beautiful machine originated in the north of Scotland.

The first engineer was Daniel Kinnear Clark. He controlled his small empire from a long distance, because he was a well-known consultant and author on railway affairs and simply served to start the railway's mechnical engineering side on a satisfactory footing. He was, after two years, succeeded by J. H. Ruthven. And four years after Clark had taken office and the railway had really begun to operate, the locomotive affairs came into the hands of William Cowan who set the most characteristic stamp upon the railway and who eventually originated the use of the 4-4-0 type which was to suffice until well into the post-Grouping period.

There were particular difficulties about the Great North of Scotland which precluded the use of anything very large and heavy. There was always some viaduct, bridge or culvert which it was not convenient to strengthen and the railway, though financially sound, could never afford to throw money away, so the locomotives were required to tread lightly upon their tracks. Cowan's earlier locomotives had some affinities with the 'Crewe' type which Alexander Allan had introduced into Scotland wherever he could. But the winding nature of the tracks soon imposed the use of a leading bogie, and Cowan, while retaining outside cylinders as did David Jones on the Highland, produced a type which was quite different in appearance. One of these locomotives survived long enough to be considerably restored to take part in the Railway Centenary Procession of 1925. Unfortunately, unlike some others which were 'revived' for that occasion, this old Cowan 4-4-0 was not preserved.

From 1883 to 1890 the engineer of the line was James Manson who came from the Glasgow & South Western, to which he returned from the G.N.S. Manson developed his

47 0-4-4 tank for the Aberdeen suburban services

admirable light 4-4-0 on the northern line. It was quite different from Cowan's, having inside cylinders. Manson also produced some eight wheeled tenders, with a bogie at the front end and four fixed wheels at the rear—a type he was also to introduce for selected services on the Glasgow & South Western. His successor, James Johnson, had only four years and generally followed Manson's precedents, but he did introduce one daring (for the G.N.S.) innovation: to this stock of 4-4-0 locomotives he introduced a 0-4-4 tank, truly a reversal of previous traditions. They were used for the Aberdeen suburban services and were as elegant as all the other small machines of the railway.

Johnson was succeeded by Pickersgill who ruled the engineering affairs for twenty years and until, in 1914, he went to the Caledonian. This designer introduced the side window cab and the graceful splasher line already mentioned, and during his superintend-ence the carriages of the railway achieved a new elegance. They had begun to be good already in Manson's time but now, apart from their shortness, they were quite the equal in style of any other carriages in Scotland, and the dark red and white livery enhanced their elegance. When Pickersgill achieved the distinction of joining the Caledonian, this was no small tribute to the quality of his work on the Great North of Scotland. It is a pity that he was by then rather an old man to undertake with complete success the far heavier responsibilities of his last appointment.

Of the Heywood era, which was the last in the independent existence of the railway, we have a charming survival in 'Gordon Highlander', which lasted in service until the years after nationalisation. Again a 4-4-0, it reminds us of the extraordinary conservatism of this railway which only departed from this wheel arrangement in a small batch of its exact reversal, and in a few 0-4-2 tanks built for working in Aberdeen Docks by an industrial locomotive builder, Manning Wardle, in 1915.

The locomotive and carriage works of the Company were long at Kittybrewster, Aber-deen, which had been the original terminus of the line before it was extended down to Waterloo Quay, the terminus until the joint station was opened in 1867. A new and larger factory was set up by Pickersgill at Inverurie in 1903.

This, then, was the small and perverse-minded Railway which eventually became sedate and well-conducted and resolved all its problems with its neighbours before losing its

48 The erecting shop at Inverurie

identity in the L.N.E.R. in 1923. Its pretty trains ran through pretty country, and consequently liberally provided with castles and gentlemen's seats of various kinds, of which one, Balmoral, near Ballater, conferred upon the line the status of a Royal Road.

The company was formed in 1845, with Thomas Blaikie as chairman and William Cubitt as engineer. The original intention of the promoters was to link Aberdeen and Inverness by a line running through Huntly and Keith, but the cost of defending this scheme against the rival Perth & Inverness Railway told heavily against the G.N.S. On 26th June 1846, the bill authorising the Great North of Scotland Railway received Royal assent, but with the company's own difficulties augmented by the national financial crisis of 1847, it was not until 1852 that the directors could authorise work to begin on the line. In 1854 a single line was opened from Kittybrewster, just outside Aberdeen, to Huntly and in 1855 a continuation was opened to Keith. A dispute with the Aberdeen Railway and the general shortage of funds were the reasons for the line beginning at Kittybrewster and continued failure to reach agreement with the Aberdeen Railway led the G.N.S. to construct its own station and its own access to the city. This line to Waterloo Quay was opened to goods and passengers in 1856.

As the G.N.S. was in such difficulties over continuing its track to Inverness and building its branch lines to Banff, Portsoy, Garmouth and Burghead, other companies stepped in to complete the work. The Inverness & Aberdeen Junction Railway, linking with the G.N.S. at Elgin and Keith, and its close associate, the Inverness & Perth Junction Railway, were amalgamated in 1865 to form the Highland Railway, but the other companies concerned all eventually became a part of the G.N.S. To the north, the line from Lossiemouth to

49 Caledonian landscape

Craigellachie was built in stages and opened throughout in 1863. From Inveramsay, two independent companies built a line to Banff and Macduff, opened in 1860 and merged with the G.N.S. in 1866, and from Dyce, on the G.N.S. main line, the Formantine & Buchan Railway built a line through Maud to the coastal town of Peterhead, opened in 1862 and extended to Fraserburgh in 1865. This line was also worked by the G.N.S. and amalgamated with it in 1866. The line from Grange to Banff and Portsoy was opened in 1859 and worked by the G.N.S. from 1863, and two branch lines, one to Old Meldrum, the other to Alford were opened in 1856 and 1859 respectively and later amalgamated with the G.N.S.

Lines were also built from Keith to Dufftown and Abernethy, opened in 1863, and from Aberdeen to Aboyne and Ballater, opened in 1859 and 1866. This latter was the famous Deeside Railway, patronised by Queen Victoria on her visits to Balmoral. It was leased to the G.N.S. in 1866 and finally absorbed by the company in 1875/6.

In this way the rail network of the Great North was built up and by 1865 three-quarters of the system was composed of subsidiary companies. To rationalise the situation an Act was passed in 1866 enabling the G.N.S. to amalgamate with its associated lines and so assume the basic form it was to retain until the Grouping. Little progress was made in linking the various networks or in any way extending the system until the 1880s because the financial crisis of 1866 had brought strict economy measures to the railway. Extensions were postponed, services reduced and maintenance work cut down to the minimum. The only important development during these lean years was the opening of the joint Caledonian and G.N.S. station in the city of Aberdeen which considerably improved the notoriously bad connections between the two railways. Previously, with the Caledonian station at Guild Street and the G.N.S. station 1½ miles away at Waterloo Quay, effecting a connection had been virtually impossible, particularly in view of the Great North's obstructive policy. The new station did not bring any alterations in the frequency or speed of the trains, there were still five services in each direction between Aberdeen and Keith, but it did mean that a passenger from the south no longer had to suffer the frustrating bus journey from one station to the other.

By 1879 the financial situation was improving and the new chairman, William Ferguson, felt able to undertake some long overdue improvements beginning with the doubling of the main line. New tracks were also laid to link Portsoy to Elgin in 1886 and Ellon to Boddam in 1897. At Cruden Bay on the Ellon–Boddam line the company acquired a large hotel and an 18 hole golf course, in an effort to popularise the area as a holiday resort, with some, but not overwhelming, success.

Better and faster trains were provided on the popular Deeside Railway to and from Aberdeen, and on the Buchan section from Dyce to Peterhead. The service to Inverness, dependent on connections with the Highland Railway, was improved in 1886 by agreement with that company, but by 1893 had deteriorated again. The agreement of 1886 for connecting services from both Elgin and Keith, brought a temporary lull in hostilities but the G.N.S. persistence in looking towards Inverness forced the Highland to end the truce in 1893. For another two years the feud continued until the Railway and Canal commissioners were called in to settle the matter. They reported in 1897, declaring Keith and Elgin to be the points of exchange between the two railways and ordering an equal number of services in each direction.

Stations at Aberdeen, Inverurie and Elgin were re-built and modernised between 1899 and 1920 and attempts were made to cater for excursion and commuter traffic. For the excursionists there were half day outings during the summer months from Aberdeen to Boat of Garten, and Aberdeen to Elgin via the Moray Firth coast. From Ballater the company operated motor buses to Braemar and from Huntly similar services to Aberchirder. It was in fact a pioneer of motor bus services, introducing them in 1904, and in the surroundings of north east Scotland such facilities proved extremely popular. By 1914 the G.N.S. had a bus route mileage of 150, that is almost half that of the railway. For the commuters, three suburban trains, one down and two up, were introduced in 1886-7 between Aberdeen and Dyce, but the demand was so great that by July 1887 the service was increased to eight trains in each direction and finally to twenty. A similar service with ten trains in each direction was begun between Aberdeen and Culter.

In spite of its small size, the company played a full part in the Great War taking coal to the minesweepers in Peterhead harbour, taking general stores to the airship base close to Peterhead and running its share of ambulance trains. Things were soon back to normal after the War and by the summer of 1919 all the fast trains, except the 6 a.m. from Aberdeen, were back on the main lines. In this way then the Great North of Scotland Railway had built itself up into a smart little concern and when it became part of the L.N.E.R. it had certainly earned its nickname of 'Little and Good'.

Printed in England for HMSO by Spottiswoode Ballantyne Printers Ltd.
Dd 736281 C 120 3/85